HOW I TRADE AND INVEST IN STOCKS AND BONDS

BEING SOME METHODS EVOLVED AND ADOPTED DURING MY THIRTY-THREE YEARS EXPERIENCE IN WALL STREET

RICHARD D. WYCKOFF

COSIMO CLASSICS

NEW YORK

How I Trade and Invest in Stocks and Bonds
© 2005 Cosimo, Inc.
For information, address:

Cosimo, P.O. Box 416
Old Chelsea Station
New York, NY 10113-0416

or visit our website at:
www.cosimobooks.com

How I Trade and Invest in Stocks and Bonds originally published by The Magazine of Wall Street in 1924.

Library of Congress Cataloging-in-Publication Data
A catalog record for this book is available from the Library of Congress

Cover design by www.wiselephant.com

ISBN: 1-59605-077-2

TO MY WIFE
Whose unfailing courage, co-operation
and belief in me has enabled me to
attain some of my ideals

CONTENTS

CONTENTS

CONTENTS

FOREWORD

During the last thirty-three years I have been a persistent student of the security markets. As a member of several Stock Exchange firms, as a bond dealer, trader and investor, I have come into active contact with many thousands of those who are executing orders and handling markets, as well as those who deal in such markets, namely traders and investors.

For the past fifteen years I have edited and published *The Magazine of Wall Street*, which at this writing has the largest circulation of any financial publication in the world.

These experiences have given me an opportunity to study not only the stock and bond markets, but all those related thereto, and have enabled me to observe the forces which influence these markets and the human elements which contribute so largely to their activity and wide fluctuations.

Out of this experience I have evolved or adopted or formulated certain methods of trading and investing, and some of these I have collected and presented in the pages which follow.

My purpose in preparing this book has been two-fold. Primarily, I have in mind the thousands of new investors who find the securities market a vast, technical machine, too complex to be understood by many. It has been my effort to do away with this impression—to emphasize the fact that, in Wall Street as anywhere else, the chief essential is common sense, coupled with study and practical experience. I have attempted to outline the requirements for success in this field in a way that will be understandable to all.

Furthermore, as I learned in preparing my first book, "Studies in Tape Reading," it is of great personal advantage for me to write out and thus clarify and crystallize in my own mind the principles upon which I endeavor to operate. And so, from both standpoints it seemed to me well worth while to arrange my impressions in methodical and coherent order.

RICHARD D. WYCKOFF.

Great Neck, L. I.
March, 1922.

I hold that a man who is long-headed, who foresees and judges accurately, has an advantage over his neighbor, and it is not accounted immoral for him to use that advantage because he is individually better fitted for the business; and it inheres in him by a law of nature, that he has a right to the whole of himself legitimately applied. If one man, or twenty men, looking at the state of the nation here, at the crops, at the possible contingencies and risks of climate, at the conditions of Europe; in other words, taking all the elements that belong to the world into consideration, be sagacious enough to prophesy the best course of action. I don't see why it is not legitimate.

Henry Ward Beecher.

How I Trade and Invest in Stocks and Bonds

FIRST LESSONS

A T the suggestion of my first employer in Wall Street, I began the study of railroad and other corporation statistics about the time my trousers were being lengthened from knee to ankle and I was receiving the munificent sum of $20 per month. This was in 1888.

With numerous interruptions my studies continued until 1897, when I began to put them into practice by purchasing one share of St. Louis & San Francisco common at $4 per share. At that time some of the other leading stocks were selling at the following prices: Union Pacific 4, Southern Pacific 14, Norfolk & Western 9, Atchison 9, Northern Pacific 11. Reading 17. To put it mildly, prices were very low. Many roads were just emerging from, or were still in, receivership, and Irish dividends were the rule.

As I saved a little money I began to buy more one share lots and finally I became such a pest in this respect that the Stock Exchange firm which I "favored" with my orders said they didn't care for the business, whereupon I decided to buy more shares, of fewer varieties.

This is the way most people begin their operations—by purchasing outright, believing that they are safe. It is true they are safe in the possession of their certificates once they have them in their safe deposit boxes, but in no other respect. They are not safe against fluctuations or shrinkages in value or earning power. Nevertheless, if their securities are well selected, and bought at the right time, the chances are strongly in favor of their making money.

It was my practice about that time to sit up nights, read the financial papers, and study probably future values of securities, and when I didn't have money enough to buy, I would make my selections just the same and write my imaginary purchases in a book with reasons alongside why they should ultimately be

worth more money. Two of these I still retain in my memory, viz., Chicago, Burlington
& Quincy at 57, and Edison Electric Illumina-
ting of New York, at 101.

I mention these incidents because they illustrate a very good way for anyone to begin to
learn the business of trading and investing in
securities. Just as in any other line it is practice that makes perfect, and most of the fatalities in Wall Street can be traced to lack of
practice. You don't have to risk real
money when you are learning, and I always
advocate two or three *years*—not two or three
months, mind you—of this kind of study and
paper practice when one is seriously considering participation in this greatest of all games.

But study and practice are the two things
farthest removed from the minds of the majority. Everyone knows that people who engage in speculation for the first time do not
want to bother with such details. The average man who comes to Wall Street comes to
speculate, although he may pay in full for his
purchases. All he asks is to be told ''something good.'' That is not speculation, it is
gambling; for speculation, to quote Thomas

F. Woodlock, "involves the use of intelligent foresight." Most people use neither foresight nor intelligence.

It might seem to the reader a long while to wait, but in my case I did not begin to invest until eight years after I started to study, and I did not commence trading for six years after that, so it may be admitted that I went to school and got a foundation knowledge which has been of inestimable value.

In connection with my one share purchases I found that although I had correctly figured financial conditions and earning power of the companies whose securities I held, their prices would often fluctuate widely as a result of general market conditions. In other words, a stock might go down, although everything in the way of intrinsic value and future possibilities pointed upward; so I made up my mind that there were other factors to be considered and found that these were principally three, viz., manipulation, technical conditions and trend of the market.

In order to study the market closely I identified myself with a leading New York Stock Exchange house which did a big business for some prominent operators, and there I learned how necessary it is to observe the proposition, not from the standpoint of the outsider who is endeavoring to anticipate the fluctuations from what he sees on the surface, but from the standpoint of the insider who is a factor in influencing prices.

Investigation proved that many of those who were thus able to affect prices often made the same mistakes as small traders, only their errors ran into big money, which, however, was not out of the proportion to their profits. Years before, in my clerical capacity in the brokerage business, I had noticed tendencies among small traders which I now found magnified many diameters in the case of large operators.

In the study of technical conditions, which was my next step, I found that the most important factor was the trend of the market and that the overbought or oversold condition of the market had the most to do with the immediate direction of the next swing.

No doubt the principles which will be found in my book, *"Studies in Tape Reading,"* were rattling around in my head for a long time before I wrote them out, and as I did this they clarified and crystallized. When I realized this, I began to put them into practice by trading in ten share lots, although I had operated in a much larger way some years before. It seemed to me that, with the right principles and a sufficient amount of practice, I could gradually build up my trading on a strong foundation that would not lead to flash-in-the-pan results but to a steady increase in speculative ability and consequent profits.

Being in the brokerage business, my immediate object was to make more money for my clients, because I realized that this was the only way in which they would become permanent and successful clients. My ultimate object, however, was to get out of the brokerage business and devote my time to the security markets, and it is a satisfaction to say that I arrived at that point some years ago.

Unlike many who operate in order that they may make money with which to enlarge their market operations, I am more interested in realizing profits so that I may have more money to invest. Just as its staff writers, through the columns of *The Magazine of Wall Street,* advocate that the business man take his surplus and invest it in sound securities, so I make a business of trading and invest the profits which result. In a word, I trade so that I may invest.

But let us go back a little and note some of the points which came to me while I was studying the subject in an objective way:

The market operations which were carried on in the office of my first employers were not significant because it was a small firm and did not have many customers. The head of the firm traded a little and made some money, because he seemed to understand what he was doing. Most of the customers, on the other hand, neither understood nor made money. Once in a while some one would come in and plunge around, pay a lot of commissions, and then go away disgusted with the business. Traders of this sort should have been disgusted with themselves. The majority seemed to look upon it as a sport or an adventure in which they hoped to prove that their judgment and ability were better than those of all who they knew had failed.

Nearly everyone seemed to be just guessing.

One man certainly carried off the palm at the business of buying at the top and selling at the bottom. Another told me how he had taken one little Reading 3rd Income Bond, worth about $300, and by pyramiding on the rise in Reading during former years had run up an equity of something over $250,000. But at this particular time he was down to a shoe-string again.

We had one old fellow who bought nothing but the very highest grade railroad bonds, and only when they were very low. Collecting these and clipping coupons was a mania with him and in order to indulge his mania he economized to the point of using a piece of plain manila twine to hold his eye glasses. He and other out-and-out investors were the most satisfactory clients because they kept coming around year after year, while those who speculated disappeared one after the other. As for the latter, I noticed a very marked tendency to accept a small profit and stand for a big loss.

About that time I heard of a prominent Brooklyn man who after several attempts at speculation said to himself, "I know the secret of this game—these traders are all taking small

profits and big losses. I will open a bucket
shop and when they do this they will force me
to take small losses and big profits.'' He did.
And in a short while he bought a couple of
hotels and was rated as a millionaire. No
doubt he mistrusted his own ability to trade as
the others were doing and followed strictly this
profitable principle (the bucket shop proprietor
may have two different kinds of principles
although they are spelled the same way), but
he knew if he got into the business he would
be obliged by the very ignorance of his clients,
to make more money than he lost.

Turning again to my brokerage office, I must
say that impressions derived there were not
conducive to speculation, but showed the
marked advantages of shrewd investing.

The next firm with which I became identified was one which had private wires, branch
offices and a considerable number of clients,
large and small. Some of them were big
traders and a few were very successful. Here
I really began to learn something from observation of their methods. The one who impressed
me most strongly was a high official of the
telegraph company from which we leased some

of our wires. He stuck out from the rest because of his fixed policy of cutting his losses short (here was that same principle bobbing up again). He never gave an order unless it was accompanied by a two-point stop. He dealt in the most active and widely fluctuating issues on both sides of the market. Unlike many of the customers who were "fluent losers" he was the only man whom I remember as being persistently successful. He would usually trade in two-hundred share lots at a time and generally managed to get a little larger profit than the two points and commission which he risked.

While I was with that firm the panic of 1893 occurred. General Electric declined from 114 to 20, and American Cordage crashed down from 140 to reorganization levels. This experience showed me what risks people ran who made speculative commitments without limiting their possible losses or watching them closely and getting out when they found they were wrong. The market for these and other stocks simply melted away, there being few buyers and many compulsory sellers. I had seen these things before in the Baring panic of 1890 but they did not make the same impression on me because I had not come into such close contact with those who were making speculative commitments of considerable size.

A few years later I secured a position with a large, ambitious and growing New York Stock Exchange house which had private wires, branch offices and correspondents all over the country. Its long list of customers and its important connections made it develop rapidly into one of the biggest houses in the Street. Here I was able to obtain a still broader view of the markets, for the concern did a big cotton and grain, as well as stock and bond, business. Many of their people made considerable money. A few made spectacular profits in a short while, but I observed that their sudden wealth led to over-extension and big losses because they evidently did not have the same judgment where larger amounts were involved. This was another point in favor of the slowly building up process.

The big wire houses in Boston, Philadelphia and Chicago poured their business over our wires, but not knowing the operations of their individual customers, I could only judge by the composite that was presented to me through having everything come in the name of the house. Two kinds of operations were evidently going on. One was a large inflow of buying and selling orders, evidently arising from those who were endeavoring to anticipate the immediate fluctuations. The result of these was indicated in a corresponding inflow of money to margin such transactions and take care of the losses which resulted in the net, proving that the traders in other cities were no different from those I had met here; that is, that they were more or loss unpracticed and inefficient at the business.

The other kind of dealings impressed me the most. They consisted of a steady line of orders to purchase securities like Atchison General Mortgage 4s, and Incomes, Norfolk & Western preferred, Union Pacific preferred, and the better grade of stocks and bonds in companies just emerging from receivership. These were bought in very large quantities and shipped away, principally to the West. Evidently there were some people in that great railroad center, Chicago, and in its tributaries, who were familiar with the railroad business, and who saw possibilities in the future for such stocks and bonds in spite of a disastrous past.

In the bull market which began with Mc-Kinley's first election in 1896, and ran for several years, these Union Pacifics, Readings, Atchisons and others which had been through receivership, reorganization and assessment, multiplied many times in value and furnished the most striking lesson I had received so far.

It was plain that the most successful class of our clients was the far-sighted investors who held, or were often able to pick up, stocks like Reading and others at less than the amount of the cash assessment that had been paid in. For these assessments they were usually given preferred stocks, and when the market prices of the latter eventually rose to around par, they had their assessment money back and either a recovery of their former losses or a big profit on the common stocks which they had acquired at the low figures.

I had a good many lessons in speculation during my four years with that firm. It being a bull period there were numerous instances of the development of small accounts into big ones. Governor Flower was the bull leader at the time and some of his stocks went from small to big figures. He had a large following, was perfectly honest with it and made a great deal of money for the public until the day he ate too many radishes at his fishing club in Riverhead, Long Island, and passed away. Next morning most of those who had made money on the bull side and had loaded up with many times what they started with lost the bulk of it at the opening.

One of my fellow clerks gave an illustration of what could be done with a little money. Starting with a small quantity of stock he pyramided until he realized the sum of $3,000, which looked very large to a thirty-dollar-a-week clerk. I found that he was not basing his judgment on the news, but on a study of the fluctuations. His specialties were American Sugar and Brooklyn Rapid Transit. Out of his profits he bought a home for himself, paying his three thousand dollars down, "so they couldn't get it away from him." He kept charts of the market and studied them intelligently, just as many other people then known as "chart fiends," were doing.

To keep charts in those days was looked upon

as making one fit for the squirrels. In and out of many brokerage offices there hustled wild-eyed individuals with charts under their arms, who would hold forth at length on double tops and bottoms and show you just where and how and why the "big fellows" were doing this or that with their favorite stocks. Yet none of them seemed to have much money. Possibly it was because they followed a strict set of rules and did not use much intelligence. It seems that the charts told them exactly what to do!

Successful students of the market were few but there were some; and I began to get a line on their methods of reasoning. I was surprised to find that the market itself did give frequent evidence of its future course and began to investigate along those lines. It did not interfere with my study of intrinsic value and earning power but rather supplemented it, for I often found that statistics and the action of the market would all point in the same direction.

So far as manipulation was concerned, it appeared to have one of three objects: Making the public buy, sell or keep out. And I judged that the manipulators were endeavoring to do the opposite. The market at that time consisted of a comparatively few stocks, although they were increasing. The dominant trading factor was James R. Keene. The Rockefeller party was active in some of its stocks. Morgan had not yet "sprung" the Steel Trust, Gates and Harriman were just coming over the horizon, and the Gould sun was about setting. It was a market which could be easily stung by a group of new powerful interests working in harmony, but while public participation and volume of trading was large, it was not to be compared with the markets of today in the number of participants or the large number of stocks dealt in.

Having secured a new angle on the market I began myself to try to judge it from its own action, principally with regard to the general trend. Dow's theory of price movement made a considerable impression on me. I understood clearly his theory that there were three distinct market movements going on simultaneously—(1) the long trend extending over a period of years; (2) the thirty to sixty day swings; (3) the small swings running from one to several days. The value of these suggestions appeared to be great when properly applied.

I thirsted for stock market and investment knowledge but much to my regret there were very few people who could assist me and very little printed matter which was of any value whatever. So I had to dig it out for myself, the best I could. It was a slow process or else I was not bright enough to absorb it quickly, but I made progress, as I will show in succeeding chapters.

MAKERS OF U. S. STEEL HISTORY

Four of the chief figures in the organization and administration of U. S. Steel Corporation whose shares have long been among the most popular investment mediums

II

HAVING accumulated enough money to go into business for myself, I resigned from the big wire house and began to deal in unlisted securities. Later on, with some associates, I formed a New York Stock Exchange firm, became the managing partner and for a number of years continued in the stock brokerage business. This put me in intimate touch with the operations of customers, and a number of other large operators.

I had not watched these traders for long before I reached three definite conclusions as to trading methods. They were as follows:

(1) The majority of those who were buying and selling securities were almost totally ignorant of the business.

(2) They were mentally lazy. They showed no desire to increase their knowledge of the subject, but anybody who gave them tips or so-

called "information" held the greatest attraction for them.

(3) Very little educational literature was obtainable, even if the trading element had been inclined to devote thought and study to self preparation.

It was astounding to see how men, shrewd, careful and successful in their own business, would come down to the Street and throw caution to the winds when they undertook to deal in stocks or bonds.

I had reached a point where I was a fair judge of the market; and I did my level best to aid them. As time went on, I did manage to help many people make considerable money; but I found that most of them wanted to lean —not to learn. They just drifted along, guided by hope of profit and pursued by fear of loss.

The clientele with which I came into contact during those years gave me a clear idea of the psychology of the average trader and investor, and I found that as a rule his viewpoint of the market was very much warped; that he did, most of the time, the opposite of what the large and experienced operator would do, because he judged by the surface conditions of the mar-

ket and not by the highly important technical
conditions. A clear understanding of these
technical conditions, I saw, was most vital to
anyone who expected to operate successfully.
And so it came about that for a considerable
time I devoted most of my thought and attention to the investment side of securities rather
than the speculative.

After founding, during the panic of 1907,
The Magazine of Wall Street, then known as
The Ticker, I began to receive numerous in-
quiries from people who were anxious to learn
more about the swings of the market, and I
also received contributions of articles from
those who had studied these subjects. Another
kind of communication contained a description
of methods more or less mechanical on which
the writers desired opinions. At that time
there was a wide interest in the search for a
method of operating which would do away with
fallible human judgment. And while this
seemed to be a species of rainbow-chasing,
there is no doubt that I was able to learn much
from a study of the different kinds of recorded
market actions. Some of the points which I
had acquired through the examination of num-

erous ideas submitted and some other points which I studied out for myself greatly aided me in judging the market.

The reason for this is tnat all graphs, charts, diagrams, etc., which form pictures of the movements of individual stocks or groups of securities, are but the concrete history of the impression of many minds upon the market. And my object in studying along this line was not to follow these indications blindly, but to see what kind of mental operations caused them. By thus reasoning out the good and bad points in the psychology of the public I hoped to get at the true method of operating.

So right here I would like to say a good word for all forms of graphs which are apt to be greatly abused and misused by people who have never taken the trouble to investigate their value. There is scarcely a business or profession today that does not employ graphs as indicators of conditions, operations, etc., in thousands of different forms. What, therefore, could be more logical than to adopt graphs as a means of seeing and clarifying such a complex proposition as the security market?

As time went on, my publication office became

the center of interest to a great number of
people who had tackled this problem from various angles, and in the examination of their
ideas and by the adoption of good and the elimination of the bad points, I gradually formed a
fairly clear idea as to how a permanent success
might be established by one willing to devote
his time and attention to the matter, making
all else secondary. As demand arose from many
quarters for information on the subject of judging the market from its own action, I decided to
make a specialty of this subject, study it out
and write about it as I went along. The outcome of this was the book, *"Studies in Tape
Reading,"* which has since been reprinted in
many editions. And the principles therein
stated have not changed through all the vicis-
situdes of the market during the dozen years
which have elapsed since the book first appeared
in serial form in *The Magazine of Wall Street.*

Many people will say it is one thing to write
about a difficult proposition like the security
market, and quite another to put your ideas into
practical operation, that is, to make money out
of them. Suffice it to say that, since I wrote
that book, I have made a very considerable

amount of money for myself and in the aggregate millions of dollars for my subscribers by applying the methods therein set forth, viz., judging from the future course of the market and of individual securities by their own action. And I expect to keep on making, each year, much more money than I spend, because the principles in that book are absolutely sound and practicable, as proven by the dollars derived from the market thereby.

In *"Studies in Tape Reading"* I suggested trading for daily profits with the object of making a fractional profit over losses, expenses, commissions, etc., on the average, per day. But eventually I found that I could get much better results by operating for the five, ten and twenty point swings. Furthermore, I learned that to operate in the latter way was to lessen the nervous strain occasioned by watching the tape every minute of the day and carrying all the quotations of the leading active stocks and their previous action in my head.

I found that the real money was to be made in the important swings running thirty to sixty days on the average, in which accumulation or distribution was clearly marked while the movement was in its preparatory stages. Experience showed that every well planned and well executed campaign in the market had three stages:

First, in the case of an upward movement, the accumulation would appear and this might run several weeks or months.

Next, would be the marking up stage, where the stock was forced upward by either bullish news or aggressive buying until it reached the level where distribution could take place.

The third stage was that of distribution.

Operations for the decline would be the opposite of this cycle.

Very often I found a stock that was being marked up would be driven far beyond the point where a substantial and satisfactory profit could be realized, but as large operators work on an average buying and selling price rather than on a definite figure, in such cases their distribution would take them on the way down. For instance, if a stock was accumulated within a range of from 50 to 60 and the objective average selling point was 80, the issue might be driven up to par and then sold on the way back to 70, so that 80 or better would be the average price received for what was sold.

These points are explained so that the reader may get an idea of how I worked out my problems, my object being to find out or reason out what the large operator did and how he did it; then I could operate in the same way, and probably with greater success. *I saw the great advantage that lay in operating with the mental attitude of the professional trader instead of the attitude of the unsophisticated outsider.*

As previously stated, I first tested out my theory by dealing in fractional lots of stocks. My progress was often halted by unexpected changes in the market, my own tendency to get away from my principles, new developments which caused me to revise many details, and lastly, the necessity for a long series of transactions which would give me a background of experience in this particular way of dealing.

Before I was really successful, I had to practically rebuild my own trading character. One of my greatest difficulties was impatience. Being of an active disposition I could not sit still long enough to allow a big profit to accumulate. In certain periods the brokers made more in commissions than I made in profits. At other times I allowed myself to be influenced by other considerations rather than the action of the market. But finally I overcame most of these faults and began to reap a real benefit from all the thought and self-training I had put into my work.

Without going into all the many details connected with judging the market, which with long practice resolved themselves into a sort of intuition, as explained in *"Studies in Tape Reading,"* it is enough to say that I have since been successful in anticipating what were apparently the turning points in the ten to twenty point swings in the market. And as every one with a knowledge of the market will understand, success in this line consists in having a greater aggregate profit over the year than the total amount of losses, including commissions, tax and interest charges.

I realize that people in general hold to the illusion that any man who can make money in the stock market should make it by the million. The public seems to think that once you know how to tap the money reservoir all you have to do is let it run. No fallacy could be more misleading.

It is true that a few large traders make spectacular profits at times. But their losses are usually in proportion, and these you never hear of. Those who make millions risk millions—often all they have on a single operation. And they frequently go broke—a condition which I never have experienced in the stock market, simply because I have never allowed myself to get into a vulnerable position. I have withstood several panics without serious losses.

Making a whole lot of money all at once is not my trading objective. I use a comparatively small amount of money in trading—not over five or ten per cent. of my loose capital—because I have no desire to spread myself out too thin, or operate in such a way that any unexpected event will cripple me. I know that there are a number of people who look upon profits as a means of enlarging their market operations. My method is to pull down the profits and invest them in safe income-paying securities, preferably those which have an opportunity to enhance in value.

There is a much greater satisfaction in operating with a small amount of money for various reasons: It makes you more careful, because, having set yourself to the task of realizing a large profit on a limited amount of operating capital, you plan your moves shrewdly and do not take risks such as you would if operating with more money. In the next place you feel that you are risking very little to make considerable. There is vastly more satisfaction in making $10,000 on a $5,000 capital than in making the same amount where $25,000 is employed.

The operations which have been the most gratifying to me are those in which I have taken, at various times, $3,000 and put it into an account in a broker's office where I could get the right kind of service at a time I expected a move of twelve or fifteen points in a certain security. One of my favorite stocks in this respect has always been U. S. Steel with which I have probably had greater success than any other issue. A few years ago, when I was very busily engaged and could not watch the market all day, I used to wait for U. S. Steel to get into position where I expected such a sharp upward or downward move and then I would buy (or sell) 300 shares, placing a three point stop order for protection. Every two points up I would buy another hundred shares, protecting each additional lot with a three-point stop. After the stock had risen about ten points I would discontinue buying. By that time I would have 800 shares. I would take my profit on a further advance or raise the stop order so that I was sure to have at least several thousand dollars profit.

In the particular year that I mentioned above, I did very little trading except for three such campaigns in U. S. Steel, where not more than $3,000 original margin was used in each campaign, but from which my net profit was about $20,000. This is what I call "good trading" because it was done with very limited risk and the profits were large in proportion to the original amount. After the first campaign, the profits were sufficient to supply the capital for the second and third operations.

Now this is not intended to convey that I, or anyone else, can continue to trade indefinitely with uninterrupted success. It merely illustrates one method of operating which has the advantages described. It always reminds me of a war-ship which, instead of turning its broadside to the enemy, shows only its bow and thus makes much less of a target. Quite a number of men in Wall Street operate in this way.

You don't hear about them, because they don't happen to be publishing magazines or writing books.   As an old friend of mine told me a few days ago, speaking of a former member of a New York Stock Exchange firm:

"He is the most successful speculator I ever met.   He will watch a stock carefully and when he judges by its action that it is ready for an important move, he will buy perhaps 500 shares. If it goes in his direction he will buy additional lots every point up, but if it should decline two or three points after he has bought it, he will throw it out immediately on the ground that his first judgment was wrong.   He has made so much money now that he takes up, and pays for, ten-thousand-share lots of stock, which in itself is evidence of what he has accomplished."

Before I go any further, let me say that not every man is adapted to trading in stocks.   In fact, very few are fitted for the work if it is undertaken as an art, a business, a profession, or whatever else you wish to call it.   One reason is that most men have a commercial training, and this unfits them for dealing actively in securities.   One of the worst traders I ever knew was a man who was highly successful, in fact, had made a fortune, in real estate. His method was to buy lots on the fringe of the city and sell them out whenever he secured a substantial profit. He applied this method to the stock market. The result was that he bought in all kinds of markets, and very often had to carry securities for months or years before he could get out. He did not realize that the tendency might change its course several times a year, and there are cross currents and counter currents which must be allowed for, which are not present in real estate.

The merchant who buys his goods wholesale, knowing that there is an established market which will yield him perhaps a ten per cent. profit after overhead and selling expenses, is also handicapped when he comes to Wall Street. One reason is that he is accustomed to buying before he sells, *whereas a man who is trading in securities should be able, ready and willing to sell short with as great facility as if buying for long account.* The merchant is familiar with the market in his own field. He judges that market by the supply and demand, and his purchases are made accordingly; but in Wall Street he does not study supply and demand because it is a very technical subject and requires close attention for a number of years before one can master it.   Even then, the best and most experienced traders have their bad times and their unfortunate seasons when the character of the market becomes too puzzling or for some reason their judgment is not up to par.

The manufacturer sells short when he takes orders for goods he has not yet manufactured. He sees orders for these goods piling up and thereupon covers his short transactions by purchasing the raw material and eventually manufacturing and delivering the finished goods; but when he enters the business of buying and selling securities, selling short is the last thing he wants to do.

From this it will be seen that special training is necessary if one is to avoid joining the ranks of those who have met the enemy and have been defeated.

Bear in mind that I am referring to the business of active trading and not to the business of investing successfully, which is an entirely different proposition, as will be described later.

Some of the principles which I have found to be advantageous in trading are as follows:

THE MAIN FACTOR IS THE TREND. If you work in harmony with the trend of the market, your chances for success are three or four times what they would be if you buck the trend. That is, if you buy in a bull market, the trend will, under ordinary circumstances, give you a profit; but if the trend of the market is downward, and you take a long position, the only way you can get out is on the incidental rally. This brief statement covers the point about as well as could be done in many chapters.

RISK SHOULD ALMOST INVARIABLY BE LIMITED. Not only the experience of those whose trading I have observed but my own experience proves that whenever one departs from this general principle he is inviting serious losses. The best way to limit your risk is to form a habit of placing two- or three-point stops behind any trade which is made for the purpose of deriving a profit from the fluctuations. Harriman contended three-eights of a point, or one point, was enough; but of course he was originally a trader on the floor of the Stock Exchange. The most successful traders have followed this rule and its importance cannot be overestimated.

ANTICIPATED PROFITS SHOULD BE AT LEAST THREE OR FOUR TIMES THE AMOUNT OF THE RISK. It must be expected that a percentage of your transactions will show a loss. The trader should aim to have such large profits on his successful trades that the losses and other expenses will still leave him something to the good. Profits can often be protected by moving stop orders up or by selling one-half of the commitment in order to mark down the cost of the remaining half. Many articles on this subject have appeared in past volumes of *The Magazine of Wall Street*.

ONE SHOULD BE ABLE TO DEAL FREELY ON BOTH SIDES OF THE MARKET. Any one who is unable to do this had better become an investor instead of a trader, buying in panics or on big declines such securities as appear to be selling below their intrinsic value.

DEALINGS SHOULD BE IN THE ACTIVE STOCKS. In order to make a profit, a stock must move. A great deal of money and many opportunities are lost by traders who keep themselves tied up in stocks which are sluggish in their action. In a commercial line you would not carry goods

on your shelves indefinitely—you would keep
your stock moving.   In trading, keep on moving
stocks!

You Should Either Make a Business of
Trading or Else Not Try to Be a Trader.
You cannot be successful at trading any more
than you can be at mining, manufacturing, doc-
toring or anything else, unless you are trained
for it.   And by "training" I do not mean an
occasional dab.   Incidentally, unless you are
peculiarly adapted to the business you had better become an intelligent investor instead of an
unintelligent trader.

E. H. HARRIMAN

One of his principles was "I am not interested in ten per cent.;
I want something that will grow"

III

WHY I BUY CERTAIN STOCKS AND BONDS

THERE is an old adage, "It is easier to make money than to keep it." I not only aim to make money, but to keep it and make it grow.

The latter is often the biggest problem of all. It involves something like defensive trench warfare. There is your back line of solid investments, bought principally for income and whatever increase in principal may result. In front of these is your second line of defense against poverty and old age, consisting of securities bought for income and profit. Out in front is your line of speculative securities which you handle so as to gain further ground, without losing your hold on your second and third line of defenses.

In choosing the better grade of securities I give serious consideration to such especially advantageous issues as equipment notes. These are known as a "pawn broker's security" because they are generally issued to secure a purchase of locomotives and cars on which a payment of ten or twenty per cent. is made by a railroad company. The balance of the obligation is paid off in annual instalments covering ten, fifteen or twenty years. As the obligation is thus annually reduced, the security for the remaining equipment grows larger and larger each year, in proportion to the indebtedness, so that toward the end of the equipment trust period the amount of the security in the shape of rolling stock increases to many hundred per cent. of the amount remaining to be paid. Equipment trusts are, therefore, to be regarded as prime investment mediums.

In spite of the many difficulties surrounding the construction and development of American railroads, I believe there is scarcely an instance where equipment bonds have been defaulted upon. Such issues are therefore well adapted to the final protection of one's investment stronghold.

Another line of income-bearing securities which I frequently favor may be found in the numerous issues of short term notes, which are excellent mediums for funds that are being put aside for specific purposes, and which will be required on a definite date. I find that their yield is often more liberal than one would expect, considering the character of the companies issuing these notes and the yield of their other securities. Due to the vagaries of the investment market, I have often picked up bargains in notes, especially those which were convertible into other securities. But one must be very careful in the selection of these, as any question as to a company being able to meet its obligations will come to the surface as the time approaches for the maturity of its short term notes.

When it comes to safe bond investments, I generally favor properties whose promise to pay is absolutely sound, but whose security is beyond question, and if possible I like, in addition, large equities such as treasury assets, as in the case of Union Pacific, oil lands, and other subsidiaries as in the case of Southern Pacific, holdings in affiliated railroad systems, as in the Pennsylvania Railroad treasury, etc.

My object in making money in securities is to have more money to invest. When I make money in the market, I don't look upon it is a means of trading in a larger way, but I consider the income that money will produce—not only the immediate income, but what in addition might be yielded from the increase in the principal if the original money is properly invested.

Long ago, for the most part, I adopted Harriman's principle which was: "I am not interested in 10 per cent. I want something that will grow." And so, in selecting securities, I try in the main to pick out those which have not small but great possibilities.

There are various kinds of investors. Some want the highest grade bonds even though the income return is small. Others want preferred stocks which yield from 6½ to 8 per cent. and which, unlike bonds, never come due, and pay their dividends indefinitely, if properly selected. Next come those investors who are willing to buy the best class of common stocks in an endeavor not only to secure dividends but to see their principal enhance in value, and are satisfied with a moderate profit.

With the major part of my available funds, I

invest in a somewhat different way, realizing that the number of years in which a man may operate successfully is limited. I want to put as much money as I can into investment channels where it will grow rapidly so that I can put the increment to work again on the same basis.

Being close to the seat of operations in the financial district I see too many opportunities for profitable investment and increase in principal to allow any substantial amount of money to remain idle. While I always have a certain amount of money in high grade investments, I have not reached the age or the stage where I think more of income than of increase in principal value. As I grow older, no doubt the proportion of securities bought for income will increase, but at age 46, as the insurance companies say, I consider that, in my particular case, it is too early for me to develop into a chronic coupon clipper.

High grade securities and coupons are, however, the proper medium for the majority of those who read this book—emphatically for those who are not experts in distinguishing

real investments and real opportunities. They
should remain in the income-only stage, so far
as most of their funds are concerned.

While there are seasons particularly advantageous for certain operations in the security
market, and while these seasons may often seem
a long time in coming, one has only to look up
the record of the fluctuations in high grade
bonds to know that once in a great while they
are on the bargain counter. December, 1919,
was one of those times, and I was not blind
to the fact. It is seldom, indeed, that one can
secure the old line, railway bonds, safe beyond
question, at such prices as were obtainable then,
and with such a long term of years to maturity.
In the belief that my investor readers may be
interested in knowing what factors convinced
me that bonds were "too low" at that time, I
append an analysis of the financial situation
as I then wrote it, and which was published in
the columns of *The Magazine of Wall Street*.

"While it is always time to buy securities for
income only, when they can be had at a rate satisfactory to the buyer, this appears to be a time
of times, and unless another world catacylsm
should occur, a duplicate of this situation may

not be seen for another ten or twenty years.

"In former years the railroads were about the only mediums for safe bond investments; but we today have a large variety of industrial and other kinds of mortgages which afford equal if not greater safety, and in many cases a larger net return.

"These are times when a man is justified in loading up with these high grade securities, that is, buying twice as many as he wants to keep permanently. This he can readily do by purchasing and paying for only half of the quantity he buys, carrying the securities in his bank, and gradually paying off the balance out of income. It matters not whether this income arises from these investments or from his business or other outside sources. Any bank with which you have dealt with will be glad to extend this accommodation; in fact, it will increase the bank's respect for your judgment.

"The present time (December, 1919) affords a rare opportunity. Such an operation should yield not only a substantial profit on the extra quantity which you now purchase, but this profit applied to the reduction of the cost of the balance of the bonds which you now acquire will so enhance the net income from the entire operation that the opportunity should by no means be overlooked.

"Never before have high grade bonds, legal for savings banks in New York State, sold so low as late in 1919. A glance over the list shows that many leading issues are selling at from ten to twenty-five points below their high figures of two years ago. Take old line investments like Union Pacific 1st 4s, having twenty-seven years to run, netting about 5.25%; Southern Pacific Ref. 4s of 1955, netting 5.45%; Norfolk & Western consolidated 4s, 1996, 5.23%; Louisville & Nashville gold 5s of 1937, 5.09%; Chicago & Northwestern general 3½s of 1987 netting 5.26%; Burlington general 4s of 1958, netting 5.43%. These are all bonds which will recover sharply in price as soon as the money situation definitely changes, and the limit of foreign government emissions has been seen.

"The Union Pacific 4% bonds of 1947, selling at about 82, are around 18 points under their market price of two years ago, and one only has to await changed conditions to see a bond of this type rise to its natural level. If this should occur in three years, the average increase in value would be 6% per annum, which, added to the nearly 5% current return on the investment should mean an annual return of about 11%. If such an advance should occupy five years, the return would be 8%. These figures spell *opportunity.*"

One field which has attracted me has been bank stocks, and the reasons were very clearly set forth in a series of articles on this subject appearing in *The Magazine of Wall Street.*

In selecting securities of banks and other financial institutions, one is in the same position as the person who is driving an automobile. He has usually three speeds in his gear case. He can travel slowly on the first set of gears, or a little faster on the second set, or very fast on "high." The institution which does an old style banking business may be likened to the first set of gears. It makes progress within a certain radius, but when a bank takes on a trust department, or a close affiliation with a trust company, making the two parts of one institution, it may be regarded as traveling on second speed. But there is still another type of institution which includes both the above and embraces an additional function which in the financial district is a very advantageous one to the stockholder. I refer to a bank which owns or is affiliated with a "Security Company" for the purpose of underwriting and conducting syndicate and investment security operations, which are, of course, very profitable.

I have been buying stocks in a dozen or more New York financial institutions. I put these in the custody of a trust company, separate from any other securities, so that dividends, rights, and stock distributions would all be paid in to this one account and reinvested in the same class of securities. My observation has shown that to secure the greatest benefit from bank stock investments, one should not spend the income derived therefrom, nor sell his rights, nor sell any stock distributions that are given, because these in time generate other melons of the same sort, and this second generation gives birth to successive series of children and grandchildren, which eventually roll up a very substantial amount of both income and principal.

In placing these securities with the trust company for safekeeping and reinvestment, I told the trust officer of the institution that this account would be in debt most of the time, because

I would buy ahead of the income and I would expect the trust company to loan whatever moneys were required for that purpose.

During the latter part of 1919 two of these opportunities developed: The Bankers Trust Co. directors recommended an increase in the capital stock from $15,000,000 to $20,000,000, the new stock to be offered to shareholders at a price of $100 per share. This is on the basis of one share of new stock for every three shares of old. Holding shares of Bankers Trust, which cost in the neighborhood of $485 per share, I was entitled to subscribe to new stock at $100, which brought the average cost down to about $389 per share.

In time these new shares will be producing other stock dividends, rights, or cash dividends, so that eventually I may have a considerable amount of Bankers Trust Co. stock. By reinvestment of income in whatever form it is distributed, the cost of this Bankers Trust Co. stock will be reduced to a very low figure.

Another case of this kind appeared not long ago in the form of a notice sent to stockholders of the Chase National Bank, which I purchased at about $675 per share. Stockholders

were asked to vote on an increase in the capital stock of the bank from $10,000,000 to
$15,000,000, with a proportionate increase in the
shares of the Chase Securities Co., which is
affiliated with the bank.   Holders were to be allowed to subscribe to one new share of the
Bank stock and one new share of the Securities
Company, for each two old shares thereof held
prior to December 26, 1919.   The subscription
price was $250 for one share of stock of the
Bank and one share of stock of the Securities
Co. I have no doubt that in time the value of all
these shares, viz., the new, which I have bought,
and the old which will sell ex-rights, will recover
to the price which I paid for the old stock, which
was $675 per share.   This means that I have
faith not only in these and the other banking institutions in which I have become a stockholder,
but in the men behind them, and in the future
of New York City as the world's banking center.

I estimate that the average return over a
period of years, allowing for rights, melons,
regular and extra cash distributions, etc., in the
leading issues is something over 12% per annum.   At this rate, my investment should

double itself in a period of something between six and seven years, allowing for the reinvestment of all dividends of every sort in the same class of securities.

The small percentage of failures among banking institutions, now that they are under such rigid control by the Federal authorities, makes their securities adapted to the conservative investor who is looking toward income enhancement and safety. My own selection included a larger proportion of shares in those institutions which have security companies attached, because these combine two companies in one, and in all cases they are being conducted with highly profitable results to the shareholders.

This taking a sum of money and planting it in a certain field without drawing down the income, but with intent to profit by its growth, may be followed out to whatever degee the investor desires. It may be begun with one share of one bank stock, or any other kind of stock or bond. It is an investment operation, but it is undertaken for income and profit, not with the idea of deriving or withdrawing that profit, but to make it yield additional sums for investment. It is a great deal like a savings bank account for the man with a small amount of cash. I remember how, with a great deal of pride, I started my first savings account with a five dollar bill (because the bank would not open an account for less), and how much satisfaction I derived from being able to add a few more fives and tens.

The man or woman who is obliged to withdraw his or her interest or, in case of a rainy day, pull down part of the principal, will be handicapped in an operation of this sort, but the object should be to make these deficiencies up when the skies again clear and to keep expenses within bounds so that the additions made annually will rapidly increase the earning power of the principal.

D. L. & W's Tunkhannock Viaduct

Showing the topography over which the Lackawanna has triumphed and typical of the immense property investment the shares represent.

IV

WHEN I buy bonds and other high grade securities for income and profit, I favor those which for special reasons are well adapted to my purpose.

First, I consider those which are selling below their intrinsic value, based on character of security. In such a case I do not lay too much stress on the interest return, although in some cases it is large. The question of marketability is important with me, however, because I prefer issues that can be instantly turned into cash. The reason for this is that always I desire always to be in a position to take advantage of a threatened panic or bargain opportunity, and as I watch the market and the general situation very closely, I frequently detect signs of trouble 'way in the distance and prepare for it.

In the case of certain 5% bonds which I hold, these are well secured, earning a big surplus, which for some reason or another is concealed.

Selling around 60, the income is very large if figured to maturity, but in selecting this bond I had my eye more on the probability that the investment public will wake up to its real value and mark its price up twenty or twenty-five points within the next two or three years. In case of an advance to 85 within three years, there would be about 8⅓% profit per annum, to be added to the flat yield of the bond. Such a 5% bond at 60, would net about 8⅓%, disregarding any re-investment of income. If, on top of this, I realize another 8⅓% in three years, the income plus profit would be 16⅔% per annum.

A class of bond which I hold and always favor, is the convertible. The advantages of convertible bonds have been too often described in past issues of *The Magazine of Wall Street* to necessitate repetition here, but if one would make a persistent study of these convertible issues, he would find every year new opportunities for making *growing investments*. Whatever is a little complicated for the average investor is apt to be overlooked and neglected. To get the best results one should be familiar with the technicalities of many kinds of con-

vertible bonds and the stipulations under which
they are issued.*   In some cases it does require
some figuring to find out just what can be done
with these issues.

For my own investment I am seldom attracted
to convertible bonds solely from the standpoint
of income, but only when I see possibilities in
the securities into which they are convertible.
In 1918 I bought $100,000 of a certain converti-
ble bond because I saw great future possibilities
in the stock into which they were convertible at
par.   At that time the stock was selling close
to the price of the bonds, viz., around 90.   Observation of the action of the bonds during the
period of weakness in the stock convinced me
that the bonds would not decline very much even
if the stock were to break ten or fifteen points,
because the investment value of the bonds kept
them up at a level where the interest return to
the investor brought in buying enough to sustain
the market price. By purchasing the convertible bonds I would have something that I need
not be concerned about, and I was sure that,
if the investment public realized the intrinsic

* These will be found in "Convertible Bonds," by Rollins,
price $3, net.

value in the stock, my convertible bonds would follow the stock along up.

This is exactly what happened. Sometime later the stock rose twenty-five points and the bonds kept a little above it, until one day the bonds were selling so much higher than the stock that I sold the bonds and bought the stock instead, thus marking down the cost of my bonds by an amount representing the difference between the price of the two securities.

This marking down the cost, by the way, is a very important factor in making investments. I keep it constantly in mind. Every investor should remember that by selling a portion of his holdings at a profit he is reducing the cost of the balance. It is good practice. I will elaborate later.

Naturally, in dealing, as I do, in all kinds of securities, there are quite a number of reasons for my going into a stock.

In 1913 or 1914 I wrote a series on "Which Kind of a Stock Is Best?" This was done as much for my own information as for my subscribers', and while I am on this subject I should like to say that I take my own medicine. In searching the security market I have a twin

purpose, viz., to find investment opportunities
for my own money and to tell my subscribers
about them.   I figure that what is good enough
for my subscribers is good enough for me.   At
the same time I wish to say that I make mistakes at times; so does everybody, no matter
how long he has been in the field.

My constant aim is to show my readers, directly or between the lines, how they may be
able to judge for themselves.   As was written
by an author unknown to me: "There are men
who will take no initiative on their own respon-
sibility, who will undertake nothing without con-
sulting others as to the feasibility of the
schemes and plans they have in view.   When a
man puts more confidence in another than in
himself he is bound to lose all will power and
become a mere dependent, awaiting orders as to
the course of action.   It is impossible for such
a man to get along in the world and make a success of his own life.   When opportunity comes
along he is afraid to seize it without asking his
neighbor's opinion."

So what I and my staff try to do is to make
our readers think and plan and carry out their
campaign in the investment field just as they do

in their own business.   This was one of my purposes in writing the series, "Which Kind of
a Stock is Best?"   As those articles progressed
they indicated that the chain store and mail order stocks were, in many respects, better than
the other leading groups such as steel, copper,
railroad, telephone, etc., the principal reason
being that these companies were putting more
of their earnings back into their business than
any other single group.

And so I bought Sears, Roebuck & Co., because its history shows that every three or four
years a stock dividend is declared.   This has
been the practice of the company for many
years.   By this method Sears, Roebuck & Co.
keep the cash in their business and use it for
healthy and profitable expansion.   The stockholder who owns a hundred shares is given
twenty-five or thirty-three shares of new stock,
which adds to his income without cutting down
the working capital of his company.   This
twenty-five or thirty-three shares additional
will, in ensuing years, probably yield another
six or eleven shares and these, in turn, will
eventually breed other little stock dividends,
all of which, added to the original shares, should

in time double the quantity of an investor's
holdings, without any further investment of
cash by him.

The purchase of a stock like Delaware, Lackawanna & Western Railroad is one which I made
for an entirely different reason.   Its dividend
yield did not attract me, but having been over
the property I realized what an enormous
amount had been expended on improvements of
far-reaching importance.   One official is quoted
as saying that they have invested, in road and
and equipment, money for expenditures that
could easily have been put off for twenty or
twenty-five years.   You may say, ''That is a
strange reason for investing in a railroad stock
when the railroad situation is so unfavorable.''
But let me tell you that when you buy into a
company like that, with enormous equities bur-
ied as a result of successful operations in the
past, you will eventually see a still greater return, because one of these days the railroads, including Lackawanna, will again come into their
own.

Lackawanna, at the end of 1918, had a profit
and loss surplus of $57,247,984 against a total
outstanding stock of $42,277,000.   In June,

1909, it declared a cash dividend of 50% out of its surplus, and a stock dividend of 15%. In November, 1911, it declared a stock dividend of 35%, payable in stock of the Lackawanna railroad of New Jersey. The system is only 980 miles long, but it is the Crœsus among railroads. From 1906 to the present time, 160 is the lowest it has sold. In May, 1919 it touched 217. Hence, when in October, 1919, I saw it decline to around 180 on a threatened coal strike, I considered it cheap, and if it should decline further I would regard it as a greater bargain.

Wall Street history shows that securities more often reach their low point when some danger or disaster is *threatened,* than upon the actual occurrence of these incidents, and the reason the low point is made just prior to, or at the time the event actually occurs, is: By that time every one who is subject to fear-of-what-will-happen, has sold out. When the thing does happen or is prevented, there is no more liquidation, and the price rallies on the short interest, or else on the investment demand created by the improved situation.

It was for these reasons that I bought Delaware, Lackawanna & Western railroad Company's stock.

Speaking of high priced stocks like Sears, Roebuck, Lackawanna and others, there is a very important reason why these are cheaper than the very low-priced stocks. Many of the shares selling in the 10's, 20's and 30's represent very little earning power. In many cases only one or two per cent. is being earned on the latter issues, with little or no prospect of dividends. Stocks paying 5 to 8% range from $60 to $100 per share. On this basis a stock paying 1% could be worth from $12 to $20. This would indicate that a non-dividend payer is worth somewhere between nothing and $12. Everything above that is hope capitalized.

Yet we have seen many non-dividend payers sell at all sorts of prices before their initial declaration. American Can, for example, sold not long ago at 68 without ever having paid a dividend. Brooklyn Rapid Transit, in 1899, sold, as a non-dividend payer, at 137; it did not make its first dividend disbursement for ten years after that.

But take the stocks selling at $200 to $400 per share and upward, and in normal times you generally find intrinsic values, future prospects, or earning power, or all combined, which justify these prices and more. Most of the very high priced stocks have hidden equities which may not benefit the stockholders right away, but which are working for them just the same. These factors may not interest the man who is long today and short tomorrow, but they do interest the permanent investor who has his eye on the development of the corporation and the future growth of the various industries and the country in general. That is why I favor high-priced stocks rather than very low-priced speculative issues.

V

SOME EXPERIENCES IN MINING STOCKS

THE investor who always chooses securities of companies who constantly put money back into their properties, will scarcely ever go wrong, but he must be constantly on the alert to notice any change in policy due to altered conditions, or to control of the property getting into other hands. The New York, New Haven & Hartford Railroad was formerly an example of progressive and conservative management and for many decades was considered a high grade investment. But the time came when a policy of expansion brought the New Haven to grief. Of this there were many signs, especially when the persistent character of the liquidation indicated that something was wrong.

Carnegie said, "Put all your eggs in one basket and watch the basket." I would distribute my eggs and watch all of the baskets.

Never get married to a security. You may

have it salted down, but there is no reason why you shouldn't freshen up your list every once in a while by going over and carefully considering what you hold and whether something else wouldn't work to better advantage for you. I find I get best results by considering each investment a separate little business enterprise. When I buy a security I figure that while as a bondholder I am a creditor and my money is secured this is not true when I become a stockholder. That makes me a partner in the enterprise and as such I want to be a live partner, not a dead one; for if I don't look after my own interests nobody else will.

That explains one reason why I like to be associated in partnership with people who are high class in every respect—because I know that they are not lying awake nights planning ways to do me or the other stockholders out of our money. Possibly no corporation head is beyond criticism, but anyone who puts his dollars into corporations like U. S. Steel, Bethlehem Steel, General Motors, General Electric and other leaders in industry and finance may rest assured that these companies are being run by the highest type of industrial captains who are intent upon making their enterprises profitable to the hundreds of thousands of big and little stockholders.

"Choose your company" is therefore a good precept for the investor.

There used to be a gang of highwaymen operating here in the Street and using the leading railroad and industrial shares as the scissors by which they parted the public from its money, but that day is rapidly passing. Leaders in finance learned long ago that they could make more money by the square deal than in any other manner. Nevertheless, I find that it pays to be sceptical until you are convinced by the past record of those in the management that they are working in your interest and not in their own.

For my own benefit, as well as that of every reader of *The Magazine of Wall Street*, I am investigating these essential factors more than ever before. It is not enough for one to know that a certain development is indicated by the surface facts and conditions—I want to get down into the root of things and find out why. For this reason I employ investigators, lawyers, mining and oil engineers. I send people to different parts of the country to get the local color and all the angles on a proposition.

After employing one engineer I sometimes send another to check him up. It might cost a few thousand dollars, but when you are putting real money into an enterprise you cannot be too sure, nor investigate too thoroughly. Not long ago I had two mining enterprises put up to me, which on a cursory examination looked good. It cost me two thousand dollars to have these properties examined, and on the engineer's reports I turned them down. In one case the mine has turned out better than was first represented to me. Either or both of these properties might develop into big mining enterprises, but taking all the facts into consideration I concluded they were not good enough for me to invest in.

While an engineer's report is by no means the last word on a property, it is a hundred times better to have an expert opinion than to take your own or some other layman's view; yet the peculiar part of mining is that even though the most eminent engineers may give an adverse report on a property, it may eventually fool them.

Mining has a great fascination for me. In fact, what came out of the ground was always of peculiar interest to numerous members of the Wyckoff family. The original Wyckoff, after landing in New York in the early sixteen hundreds, had charge of Peter Stuyvesant's estate, which was located in downtown New York, where the Hudson Terminal Building now stands. His descendant, my grandfather, who organized the Hanover Fire Insurance Co., and was one of the original interests in the Hanover National Bank, was also deeply interested in mining. He invented a separation process back in the fifties and successfully mined gold in the State of Virginia before and during the Civil War near where the Battle of the Wilderness was fought.

If I had my business career to plan over again, I would be inclined to favor mining engineering, for it is an interesting profession; but in visiting numerous mining properties and watching the methods of engineers and the difficult conditions which often prevail in the different mines, I can readily see how Old Mother Earth can fool the best of them. For that reason I never go into a mining enterprise unless I am prepared to lose every cent I put into it.

But there are many ways in which even a layman can check up such an imposing person as the mining engineer. I have made considerable money in mining stocks, and I expect to make a great deal more because I have learned a lot thus far and will use what knowledge I have to better advantage in the future.

First of all, I want to know who are the interests behind the mine—whose dollars are alongside of mine? Have they a record for successfully developing other mining enterprises? What mistakes have they made? Were they fooled themselves or did they fool the stockholders—which or both? Along what line is the development work now proceeding? Is the company properly financed? What is the character and reputation of the engineer who is guiding the development work? Is the metal or mineral which they are producing such that an advantageous market is afforded now and at all times? If it is a gold, silver or copper mine, what is the outlook for those metals? Are future conditions so shaping themselves that the mine can be regarded as more or less of a manufacturing and therefore an investment proposition? Is the nature of the ore such that it will peter out within a few years or is there a certain deposit of ascertainable value which can be diamond-drilled and its value estimated? Under these conditions, what is the probable life of the mine and the estimated profit per share during that period? These and dozens of other questions are what I ask myself and others before putting my money into a property.

Some mines are highly speculative; some are at or approaching the investment stage. My problem is to get aboard the best of them before they get to a stage where the cream is all off. In other words, I want some of the cream, and in order to get it I frequently have to go in early and sit in for a long time before the skimming process can be accomplished.

Sometimes I go into a mining stock in order to derive a profit from the fluctuations in the market price, and other times to get my profit out of the ground. In order to illustrate this point I will explain an operation in Magma Copper, which stock I have held in substantial quantity for over four years.

I was coming downtown one day when a friend whom I met told me there was "something doing" in Magma, and suggested that I watch it. I did watch it, and saw that careful buying was proceeding. (I always lay more stress on the action of the market than on what anybody says.) As I remember, the stock originally came out at about $12 per share, rose to $18, then sold off to around $15. When he told me this it was up to $20, indicating that new influences were at work.

I decided to buy 200 shares and await further developments. The price hung around the same figure for a day or two, when suddenly my broker called me up and said Magma was 21 bid, whereupon I immediately gave him an order to buy 500 shares at the market. He had to pay 22 for some of it. I then bought another 500 shares, which cost me a point or so higher. As I always like to buy something that is "hard to purchase," the action of this stock pleased me very much, especially as it closed that night around 28 or 29.

Then I set out to find what it was all about, and I learned that the character of the ore in Magma had been discovered to be such that if it was present in any great quantity the mine would be one of the most important in this country, for insiders would then consider it worth $200 per share. So I told my friends about it.

No doubt the bucket shops were heavily short of this stock, because when the urgent buying continued, the price rose rapidly, until in about three weeks it sold at 69, and I had about $55,000 profit on my 1,200 shares.

Did I take this profit? I did not. I did not go into it for that amount of money. Have I been joshed about not taking it during the time the stock has wiggled back and forth between 25 and 55 for the last four years? I have. Why did I not take it? I'll tell you: Because when I bought that stock I resolved that more money was to be made out of the mine than out of the fluctuations—unless someone was lying. And following my usual resolution to be prepared for the loss of whatever I put into any mine, I made up my mind to sit with my $23,000 investment in Magma until it proved to be either a fake or a bonanza.

It has proved to be a bonanza, and although the stock is today selling for only one-half of its high price of 69, I not only have the same opinion of its future as was indicated in 1915, but I have many, many more reasons, for believing in the soundness of the enterprise.

Magma Copper Company is capitalized at $1,500,000 authorized, and $1,200,000 outstanding stock of $5 par value. There being only 240,000 shares, a price of 35 represents a market value of $8,400,000. The leading interest is Col. Wilzam B. Thompson, who, in the last twelve or fifteen years, has made more millions in mining securities than any other man in Wall Street.

Ever since the real value of the property was discovered Mr. Thompson and his friends have been steadily accumulating Magma, until now, out of the 240,000 shares, there are not more than 20,000 shares in the hands of the public. How do I know this? Because I have gone to very great trouble and expense to check it up from various angles. I am not taking anybody's word; I have got at the *facts,* not only from a Wall Street point of view. A few months ago I visited the property, and with my mining engineer went down to the 1,400-foot level. I saw 40% to 60% bornite on all sides of me in some of the tunnels and cross-cuts.

The property is being developed on a tremendous scale, and now that its new shaft has been completed, it is ready for quantity production. Its silver and gold values so reduce the cost of its copper that it is one of the lowest priced producers in this country today. And down below there is a world of ore.

Those who know Colonel Thompson best say he will never sell his Magma. For my part, I intend to wait until I see him start to distribute, and then they can have mine.

Carping critics will say, "He's trying to boost Magma, so he can sell it." Let them carp. I don't care whether anyone who reads this buys Magma or not. It makes no difference either to Colonel Thompson, to me, or to my friends and subscribers who have bought the stock on the strength of what they have read in *The Magazine,* and who hold most of the 20,000 shares to which I have referred. All I wish to say to them is: Hold it, and you won't be sorry. As for professional parasites and self-appointed critics, let me call their attention to the fact that I talk, write, investigate, trade and invest in nearly all securities on the New York Stock Exchange and outside at one time or another.   Hence, criticisms may as well be prepared in advance and arranged alphabetically for easy and prompt access when required.

This experience in Magma illustrates the advantage of thoroughly investigating and then sticking to your holdings like grim death, or until something occurs which, for a definite reason, causes you to change your position.   I do not claim that the paper profit in Magma thus far is any criterion, but I wish to emphasize the importance of making a resolution in connection with investment or speculative transactions and basing that resolution on sound premises—making of them a sort of statistical rock upon which you may place your feet and stand there indefinitely.

Lots of people have said, "Why didn't you sell out and buy back cheaper?"   Personally, I have never made any money by trading backward, by which I refer to the hind-sight which is so frequently flourished in Wall Street as an indication that the flourisher is blessed with an acute foresight.

Had I sold at the high price, I could of course have bought back on a scale down, or a lower figure, then re-sold and re-bought, but as I have said, I was not in that kind of an operation, although it took considerable strength of purpose to resist at times. Ore in the ground, when combined with first-class management, ample capital and big personal commitments on the part of those who are running the property, is about as safe as money in the bank; but it must be the right kind of ore and in such quantity that it will yield a very large return in proportion to the orginal investment.

Elsewhere the reader will find reference to the difficulty in waiting for a big profit, but in the main people have less trouble with their patience when they face a large loss. There is one way in which most of this difficulty can be overcome, and that is by carefully assembling the facts when you enter a commitment and continually checking up all along the line for the entire time that you hold it. There is no need for guess-work, if one will take the trouble. It is merely a question of how much labor and expense you are willing to go to in order to make your investment successful.

We succeed in proportion to the amount of energy and enterprise we use in going after results. Success is not for the man who is willing to sit down and wait for something to fall into his lap.

It is poor policy, I find, to wait for Opportunity to knock at your door. I train my ear so that I can hear Opportunity coming down the street long before it reaches my door. When Opportunity knocks, I try to reach out, grab Opportunity by the collar and yank it in.

FIFTY YEARS
AGO

TO DAY

JOHN D. ROCKEFELLER

Whose fortune of nearly one billion dollars represents investments, for the greater part, in the necessities or near-
necessities of life

VI

THE FUNDAMENTALS OF SUCCESSFUL INVESTING

ONE of the most important considerations when making an investment is to understand the nature and condition of the industry which that security represents. Look over the mediums which John D. Rockefeller and others of his family select, and you will find that they are mostly in the necessities of life—oil, gas, food or other near necessities, such as iron, steel, harvesting machinery, etc. These are branches of endeavor in which there is an already created and continual demand—human need of fuel, light, eatables, or materials necessary to produce them. It is a good point to bear in mind.

As I get deeper and deeper into this problem of making money in securities, and then making the securities make more money, new avenues for thought, research and investigation are constantly developing. Of late I have been more than ever impressed with the importance of understanding the present condition and future tendency of the industries represented by the multitudinous corporations whose shares are listed or unlisted in New York and elsewhere. It was for this reason that I established in *The Magazine of Wall Street* a department known as Trade Tendencies. This feature is worthy of careful study.

While in former years I usually began with a consideration of the trend of the market, and then passed to the choice of security, I now line the factors up in the following order:

(1)   Long trend of the market.

(2)   Nature and tendency of the industry.

(3)   Trend of the selected company's affairs (toward improvement or contrary).

(4)   Character and reputation of the management.

(5)   Financial position and earning power.

(6)   Position in relation to the intermediate, i. e., the thirty to sixty-day swings.

When all of the above prove up to my satisfaction I feel safe in making an investment.

Of course, there are other considerations, but these are the most important.

Practically everyone agrees, and I have proved in another series of articles, how vitally important it is to know the long trend of the market. This is the compass by which all courses should be steered. It is so fundamental that there is little ground for discussion, but I may say that it is one of the main points in successful investment. The reason is that even when a purchase is not well-timed, it is likely to show a profit at sometime or other if the broad general tendency of prices be upward. Even poor weak stocks advance to some extent in a bull market. On the contrary, if a person buys a stock in a bear market, he is likely to have to carry it a very long while. If it be in a weak financial position, he may have to see it through a receivership, or he may decide to sell out at a big loss in order to save what little remains. From this it will be seen how important is knowledge of the long trend.

Suppose I have decided that the automobile industry is in a very sound, prosperous and promising condition, and I am considering an investment in one of the best of the automobile companies' shares. I would not feel justified in making this investment unless satisfied that the long trend of the market is upward. The action of the market discounts the business situation six months to a year in advance; prices of stocks point farther ahead than any individual can see, and because these prices represent the combined or composite opinion of the millions of people who are dealing in securities. They express themselves by their purchases and sales; hence a study of the tendency of the general market and of individual stocks is a study of the minds of men.

Therefore, when I decide that the automobile industry is in a favorable position, and that the long trend of the market is upward, I set about to select the company engaged in that industry; then I determine (a) whether the tendency of its business is toward improvement or to the contrary; (b) character and reputation of the management; (c) financial position and earning power; (d) position of the stock or bond in relation to the general market and its position in the intermediate swings (if it be a stock) represented by the thirty to sixty-day movements in prices.

It is not claimed that I go through any set formulas, but this is the general plan of reasoning which I follow, and which, through long association with the various kinds of market securities, financial statements, management, and periodical swings in prices has become almost instinctive, so that it takes me only a short time to make up my mind that a proposition measures up to my requirements.

At the beginning, of course, I had to sit down like anybody else and pore over a mass of data and statistics and look up records just as a lawyer, doctor, or anyone else has to do when he first begins to practice. But trading and investing is like any other pursuit—the longer you stay at it the more technique you acquire, and anybody who thinks he knows of a short-cut that will not involve "sweat of the brow" is sadly mistaken.

Pertaining to the matter of condition and outlook for the industry in which I might be considering a venture, I want to show how it should take precedence over many other factors which are included in the examination of a contemplated investment. When I first came down to Wall Street, there was practically only one industry represented on the New York Stock Exchange—that of railroading. Everything revolved around the state of the crops, because wheat, corn, oats and other crops were the country's mainstay, and most of the speculative campaigns by large operators like Gould, Keene, Philip Armour, Deacon White and others, started with the crop outlook as the base.

That condition has changed. We have many hundreds of industries represented by the listed and unlisted securities that are now freely dealt in by investors, and this list is being added to every week. So, while the railroad stocks are still a factor, there are more oils than rails and a great many more motors than there used to be. All these groups are subject to various influences which affect their respective industries, and in many cases their industries are so intertwined that prosperity or depression in some is bound to bring about a similar condition in others.

The automobile industry is a striking example of this. If, as one high official has stated, there is a latent demand for two million automobiles, it means that there exists a like possibility of expansion in the rubber tire, steel and oil industries. Another instance is found in the rails. The roads having been handed back to their owners, once their financial position and earning power is assured, there will immediately spring up an unprecedented demand for railway equipment. This in turn would favorably affect the steel industry, because the railroads are such very large consumers of rails and other equipment requiring the use of steel.

Then comes the secondary consideration of the effect of prosperity in these lines upon other industries. Included in automobile manufacture must be literally hundreds of allied lines such as concerns making bodies, tops, radiators, motors, wheels, etc., now that the indirect effect of a prosperous condition in the automobile trade is disseminated through thousands of different channels.

The two factors above named have a still greater influence upon the spending power of the millions whose earnings are kept at a high level by reason of the demand for labor and materials, and what is known as the spending power of the public runs into thousands of trade

avenues, resulting in a great stimulation of all
lines of industry.

Perhaps I have got away from my subject
a little, but it is interesting to follow a thought
towards its logical conclusion.

The above condition therefore brings about,
directly and indirectly, a stimulation of various
lines, while in other industries, working under
adverse conditions, the effect is contrary; hence
we must conclude that there are numerous tendencies going on in the market all the time,
some being reflected by higher prices for these
groups of securities, while prices of other
groups are declining. This will make clear
why it is so important to study the various lines
of business in order to choose, by a process of
elimination, those which are likely to show the
best results, even if conditions in other lines
are somewhat unfavorable. I have seen cases
where the progress of a certain industry more
than offset the declining tendency of the general
market, resulting in certain stocks going up
while most others were going steadily downward. When I can make an investment in
which the condition of that trade is ideal, and

when the long trend of the market is strongly upward, with all the above-named factors satisfactory, I feel rather certain that the outcome will be profitable.

These points being settled, the next step is to decide what stock in that industry is in the best position as regards earning power and financial strength, character and reputation of management, etc.   From an investment standpoint the above factors should dominate, but from a speculative standpoint, the matter of technical position would have almost equal weight.

In selecting a stock for income and profit, or choosing one which I buy primarily for profit, I always like to choose the one which will make the greatest amount of money for me in the shortest length of time.   This is where a study of technical position comes in.   A certain stock may look good to me because it has risen from 100 to 150 and then reacted under an assault by the bears (but without any especial change in its fundamental position, outlook or earning power) to a price of 110.   If it shows at that level strong resistance to pressure, I would much rather buy it than some stock which was still in the range of distribution after being marked up 40 or 50 points and made very active around the top. These are but simple examples of a study of the action of different stocks and some of my reasons for choosing one rather than the other after giving due weight to all the other factors in the case.

It is strange how people will continue to ignore the important elements just referred to. Probably it is because they do not understand the operations that underlie the fluctuations in securities and which are responsible for many of their movements. I refer to the campaigns mapped out and carried out by pools consisting of groups of a few or many men who look far ahead and observe the approach of a situation which will enable them to buy or sell to advantage.

As Charles H. Dow used to say: "The public rarely sees values until they are pointed out,"—which means that the public does not lead, but is led in speculation. It rarely acts until it is told to act, or until action of some sort is suggested by a bit of verbal information, a market letter, etc.

But there is another kind of suggestion which is the most potent in its influence on the public, and that is the action of the market itself. A rising price for a stock suggests still higher prices and declining quotations bear the inference that prices are going lower. Pools work on this weakness, which is due to ignorance on the part of the public. They accumulate a stock without advancing its price; then, when market conditions are favorable, they bid the stock up. This excites public buying, because people always want to get in on something that is "going up." Vice versa, groups will often try to depress a stock, counting on the public's support when the issue begins to decline.

It long ago occurred to me that success in the security market demanded an understanding of the operations of those who were most influential, because these interests had been studying the business and operating in the market for many years and were therefore experts. It was sound reasoning to suppose that a knowledge of the principles which they used in their market operations would enable one to detect their thumbprints on the tape and to follow with pleasure and profit.

Large interests are practically always in the market. They usually have their scale orders in on both sides so that they buy on declines and sell on rallies. They always have money with which to buy on declines, because they sell on the rallies. They thus realize a profit as well as supply funds for the next decline. If the public would learn to do this, there would be fewer stock market fatalities.

It is difficult to over-emphasize the importance of studying the technical position, particularly when making a speculative commitment. Many people may say, "What is a weak or a strong technical position?" My reply is, in brief, that a stock is in a weak technical position on the bull side when it has been purchased and is held by a large number of outside speculators; when most of these are looking for a profit; when the price of the stock has advanced to a point where no further buying can be stimulated for the time being. It stands to reason that when buying power is exhausted a stock must decline, no matter how strong its finances, management or earning power.

On the other hand, a stock is in a weak technical position on the short side when the bears have exhausted their ammunition by selling all they can afford and when the buying power of investment and speculative purchasers is such that it resists the pressure of the bears; in other words, when demand overcomes supply. The weakness in such a position is found in the fact that all those who are short are potential bulls; they must, sooner or later, cover their commitments in order to close their trades. They do not wish to remain short indefinitely. It is a well-known fact that bears have less courage than bulls, and they are often obliged to buy at higher prices because the technical position becomes so strong that they cannot force the price lower. Bears, after they have sold short, are an element of strength, not of weakness.

Much could be written on this subject, which, while far from being an exact science because of the numerous and changing influences that are being thrown into the market at almost every moment, is a study which well warrants the attention of every investor and trader.   The old adage "well bought is half sold" should always be borne in mind, and while this study of the technical position is a point which people get around to last, one's security market education is not complete without it, nor can it be mastered without patient study, long experience and practice.

There are many men in Wall Street and throughout the country who make a practice of taking profits in accordance with their ideas of proportion, something like this: They say, "Fifty points is a big profit, even if it is on a small lot of stock; therefore, I will take it." Others say to themselves, "I have a profit of a hundred per cent on my investment and that's good enough. I will let someone else have the rest."

In the case of American Graphophone, I followed a different rule. The number of points, or the percentage of profit, did not influence me. The fluctuations were interesting, but whether the stock went up or down, I decided to wait for it to reach a certain point before I would take profits. This meant the point where the insiders began to sell.

VII

THE STORY OF A LITTLE ODD LOT

IN previous articles I have referred to the importance of a thorough understanding of the industry represented by the security in which you have decided to invest. One cannot place too much emphasis on this point. Some people, when they look at the list of securities quoted in the dailies, do not know whether the abbreviated titles refer to railroads, industrials, or billy-goats. But they ought to know and especially should they be acquainted with the history, finances and character of management of their chosen enterprises.

For a long time I have been familiar with the history and development of the phonograph industry, and have made calculations as to its future trend. For many years it was largely monopolized through the protection of patents which some people disputed but which were at any rate effective. And so when in February, 1919, I was having lunch with a friend, and he told me something important was likely to come out of the approaching meeting of the American (now Columbia) Graphophone Company, I knew that back of any immediate development in that company's affairs there was a solid foundation for what might occur.

We were discussing how the millions of soldiers who went to the war were coming back music-crazy, and how their experiences abroad and in American camps proved to them the value of the phonograph in the home; how people who never before could afford such luxuries were now able to buy, resulting in an unprecedented demand for both machines and records.

"I understand," said my friend, "that the announcement to follow the Columbia meeting is likely to put the stock to 150."

As the issue was then selling around 135 I did not pay much attention to it, and had almost forgotten the incident when one morning, coming down to the office, I noticed in my newspaper a small announcement to the effect that the Columbia directors had declared a dividend

of $2.50 per share in cash and one-twentieth
of a share in stock.   Elsewhere in the paper,
among the obscure news items, it was suggested that it would be the policy of the Graphophone Company in future to disburse a certain amount of cash every quarter and a
small stock dividend as well. Both the
official anouncement and the small news item
were couched in such modest terms that the
significance thereof did not appear on the surface.

But a little mental calculation worked out
like this: $2.50 per share per quarter meant
$10 a year. One-twentieth of a share per
quarter was four-twentieths, or one-fifth of a
share per annum.   At the market price of the
stock, 135, this one-fifth of a share equals $27
per share per annum, or a total of $37 per
share—counting cash and value of stock—dividend. Conclusion: The price should advance
from $200 to $300 per share, dependent upon
how certain the regularity of the stock dividends intended to be paid.

Upon reaching the office I phoned the company's headquarters and found that the management planned to declare these quarterly

stock dividends at the one-twentieth rate indefinitely, so I started to invest at least $15,000 in American Graphophone common at the market price.   Evidently other people were awake to what that little announcement meant, for there were lots of buyers and few, if any, sellers.   I finally succeeded in buying two twenty share lots, averaging 164¼, and the next that was offered to me was around 179. As this was a long way from the price at which I started to buy, and I didn't like to bid up against so much competition, I decided to give the forty shares to my wife and to see what I could do for her with the little odd lot.   Soon the price was 180, then 200 bid, with hardly any transaction in the meantime.

These forty shares of stock cost $6,575, which, while not much of an investment, had great possibilities, considering its size, as I will show. It was not my first transaction in Graphophone, for I had made considerable money in it on previous occasions, buying it around 70, selling at 135, re-buying around 110, and carrying it up to 160.   Considering these transactions, the forty shares cost me much less than nothing.

About five years ago *The Magazine of Wall*

Street published an article on the phonograph industry, which showed it to be in a very prosperous condition with an outlook that was exceptionally promising. A certain New York stock broker, knowing that the stock of the old American Graphophone Company had been well distributed many years before, and that control was to be had in the open market, went to Wilmington, Del., and succeeded in obtaining a fifteen-minute interview with the du Pont interests. The upshot of this was that the du Ponts acquired control, buying the stock from below par up to nearly $200 per share for the last of their stock.

Then began a period of development and expansion under the new and more progressive management. In consequence, the company had made very great strides in the last few years. During this time the stock, which had reached 196 or thereabouts, gradually declined, until in the summer of 1918 it was selling around $50 per share. Somewhere between that level and the 135 figure which prevailed when my attention was again called to it, those in control evidently saw an opportunity to "put

it over big," just as they had in General
Motors and other large corporations in which
they were interested, with a resulting scarcity
of stock when the news came out.

I knew that the new corporation which had
recently taken over the old was supplied with
an issue of common stock far in excess of
what was to be used in the exchange for the
old shares, and in this dividend announcement I read between the lines and was able to
forecast much more accurately than if I had
not been familiar with the past history of the
Columbia, and had not studied du Pont methods
of financing and development.

In the previous chapter you will find a reference to the technical position. It would be
difficult to imagine one stronger than that pre-
vailing in this stock after the news came out,
because, in simple Wall Street parlance, "there
was none of it for sale." And it was not long
before the stock sold at over $300 per share.

During the summer, while I was on a long
trip to Alaska and the Coast, I used to get the
New York papers from seven to fifteen days
late, but I knew that anything big or important

would take several weeks to consummate, so I would have ample notice.

With frequent resting spells and reactions the stock climbed steadily to $400, and then to $500 per share, and with each fresh advance the stock dividends which were being distributed quarterly became more valuable; that is, the one-fifth of a share per annum (consisting of four quarterly payments of one-twentieth of a share) had a value of $40 per share when the stock sold at $200; $60 per share at $300; $80 per share at $400; and $100 per share when the price advanced to $500. It was the closest thing to "lifting itself by its boot-straps" that I had ever seen.

On the 40 shares the first dividend amounted to 2 shares; the second to 2.1 shares, making 44.1 shares. By that time the shadows of coming events began to show, for the company announced that it would shortly exchange the old stock of $100 par, for new stock of no par value, and that each holder of one share of old would receive ten shares of new stock. Occasional transactions on the Curb had been in the neighborhood of $500 per share, and now the new stock began to be traded in "when issued" between 43 and 50, and during the month of August, 1919, ran up as high as 59. At the low level of 43½ to 46 during August and September the stock showed excellent resistance, while the rest of the market remained weak, and from its action I came to the conclusion that we were approaching the "fire-works" stage.

Along in October the stock was listed on the New York Stock Exchange and began to be very active, advancing rapidly several points per day until it reached 75. The volume of trading greatly increased. In some sessions there were from 50,000 to 75,000 shares dealt in, to say nothing of the odd lots which were not recorded. Numerous newspaper articles called attention to the company's development. I watched it work back and forth between 70 and 75, and when I saw certain indications appear, made up my mind that if it again declined to 70 I would sell part of what once was an odd lot.

The 44.1 shares were by that time exchanged for 441 shares of new stock, and soon afterward a dividend of a fraction over 22 shares

was received, making 463 shares, worth $70
per share $32,410.00
Plus three dividends at $2.50 per
  share on various lots 315.25
                                     _____
                                     $32,725.25
Less cost of original 40 shares and
  commissions 6,575.00
                                     _____
Paper profit at $70 per share $26,150.25

The stock dividends which were coming along
quarterly amounted to 23 shares or $1,610 worth
per quarter, or $6,440 per annum if the stock
remained at $70. Add to this the cash divi-
dends, which, on the new stock amounted to
one-tenth of the old, and were being paid at
the rate of 25 cents per share, or $1 per annum,
the income amounted to about $6,900 on an
original investment of less than $6,600.

That was a big percentage, provided the stock
stayed at $70 per share, but the action of the
stock indicated that insiders were selling at
least a part of their line, perhaps enough to
get back their original investment. Deciding

that when insiders sell it is time for outsiders to sell, I disposed of 263 shares at 70, which gave back the original $6,575, besides $12,080.25 in cash, in addition to 200 shares paid for in full.

In fact, allowing for the profit and cash dividends, these 200 shares cost about $60 a share less than nothing. So I didn't see how my wife could lose on that transaction.

Selling part of the lot put me in a good position for another reason. If the insiders were to support the stock on a decline, then lift the price to a new high level, I could take advantage of it with the remainder of my holdings. But if, as was more likely, they allowed the stock to sag off, I could replace what I had sold at a lower level and then take advantage of any secondary advances and distribution that might occur.

The points to bear in mind in regard to this little deal in odd lots are these: I knew the industry, its present over-sold condition and its future trend. Also the position of the Columbia Company with relation thereto.

Inside information said the stock would advance 15 points. It was wrong; the price rose hundreds of points. The information on which I really acted was open to everyone. I confirmed the facts at the company's office.

By putting myself in the place of the insiders I was able to follow their reasoning and see the purpose behind their campaign. I took profits when they did, thus placing the account in a strong cash position, beyond the possibility of loss.

Surface or present conditions were not considered, but only the facts which indicated what the future would be. Technical conditions were closely watched for signs of moves by the insiders.

Selling around the top provided the cash with which to replace at a lower figure.

I did not get a full hundred per cent. of the possibilities in this little deal, but came mighty close to it.

My experience with American Graphophone shares show what can occasionally be done with odd lots, and disputes those who believe that fractional lots of stock are too small to bother with and should be ignored. I have described the matter in detail so that the reasons for every move are clearly set forth, and trust that the suggestions herein will be found of suggestive value to my readers.

JESSE L. LIVERMORE
Whose stock market operations are the most spectacular in
the present generation.

VIII

SOME people may form an impression, based on my previous articles, that when one acquires the proper amount of training and experience, making money by trading and investing in securities is an easy proposition. I hasten to correct either this impression or another which might also have been formed: that it is easy sailing for me personally.

I have yet to find the man, in or out of Wall Street, who is able to make money in securities, continuously or uninterruptedly. My experience is no different from that of many individuals who are known as successful Wall Street men. Like every one else, I have my good and bad periods. Sometimes it appears as though everything I touch pans out well, and at other times everything seems to go wrong. It is much like any other line of business.

Success in trading means an excess of profits over losses.   Success in the investment field means more good than bad investments.   If any one tells you he can be almost invariably successful, put him down as trying to impose on your credulity.   One hundred per cent. accuracy was a height not even attained by the late J. P. Morgan.   James R. Keene often said he was doing well if he could be right six times out of ten.   I often used to call on him and watch him trading over his ticker on the fifth floor of the Johnson Building, 30 Broad Street, and there was many a time when I could plainly see from the nervous way in which he worked back and forth from his ticker to his telephone, and paced up and down the floor like a caged lion, that things were not going well.   In his thirty or forty years, Wall Street career he went broke more than once.

I went into Harriman's office one day and found him a veritable bull in a china shop, because the market had been going contrary to his expectations.

In the present generation Jesse Livermore's operations are the most spectacular, but he is not by any means always right.   Like all other traders, big or little, he makes serious mistakes at times. He has personally described to me his methods in detail. They provide for mistakes, accidents, errors in judgment and those unexpected happenings which every big or little operator must allow for.

One of the cleverest and most experienced traders on the floor of the New York Stock Exchange—a man who usually makes $300,000 a year out of his floor trading—said to me, "Whenever I take a position in a stock and find that it is running into a sufficient loss to amount to $20,000 or $25,000, and it begins to bother me in my day-to-day trading, I close it out."

Now go into the investment field and take the published annual list of investment securities owned by any of the big life insurance companies such as the Equitable, Mutual, New York Life, or others who have the very best connections in the financial district, and whose investments are made under the advice and guidance of eminent financiers, attorneys, experts and actuaries. You find the same thing—frequent investments which turn out badly and which have to be written down and charged off.

Success in either field, therefore, depends

upon whether your profits exceed your losses and income—how close you can come to one hundred per cent. accuracy. So no matter how long or how hard you study, nor how careful, conservative and experienced your guide, your counsel or your bankers, you must anticipate a certain portion of unfortunate investments and operations.

It is for this reason that many (but not all) of my investments are made with intent not only to realize large profits but to offset these occasional and unavoidable losses. I have found some men who claim that they never take a loss. This may be true, but I would rather take losses than take an inventory of the final result of such operations, because it is bound to show a number of securities that are miles away from their cost and which should be listed merely either as "Hopes" or "Faint Hopes."

This reminds me of a very clever trading rule followed by Jesse Livermore. Unless a stock shows him a profit within two or three days after he buys or sells it short, he closes the trade, on the ground that his judgment was wrong as to the immediate action of the stock,

and he cannot afford to be tied up.   He says,
"Whenever I find myself *hoping* that a trade
will come out all right, I get out of it."

Livermore's purpose in this rule is to keep his
trading capital in circulation; never allowing
it to become congested.   It is a good rule.
Think it over, and you will recall that you
have often not only lost money by sticking to
a hopeless proposition, but you have lost many,
many opportunities.

Another Livermore principle is the cutting
of losses.   Of course, in his 10,000, 20,000 or
50,000 share campaigns he cannot place stop
orders like a 100, 200 or 500 share trader, but
he usually has a mental stop and when it is
reached he closes out the trade.

It will be observed that Livermore, by the
use of these two rules, has both a time and a
price stop.   He will not devote his margin (capital) to a transaction for more than a few days,
and he will not let the trade run against him
for more than a few points.   While he, so far
as I know, originated the first rule, the
second, viz., the use of stop orders, has been
one of the first principles of successful opera-

tors for many years. Harriman, Keene, and a host of others have advocated the absolute limitation of risk.

While I have made it a practice to limit my risk in most cases, I can trace most of my principal losses to my failure to place stop orders when the trades were made. And while I have always studied the limitation of risk and generally endeavored to trade in a way that will keep the risk down to a minimum, I have very often delayed placing a stop order until the opportunity was lost, and in some cases these losses have run into five or ten points when they might just as well been limited to two or three. These incidents are of value because they show what should be avoided.

In trading I get the best results by watching carefully for an important turning point, limiting my risk, and trading for the ten or twenty point swings. But very often when I have the time to devote to it, and I feel myself in harmony with the market, I like to trade actively. Jumping in and out of stocks to the extent of 5,000 or 10,000 shares a day in the aggregate is a lot of fun, but is usually more profitable for the broker than for the trader, because of the immense handicap he is under in trying to pay commissions, taxes, and losses out of the small daily swings and get a profit besides. A trader on the floor of the New York Stock Exchange has an advantage over a non-member, whose total expenses on such business under the increased commission rates run from $1,000 to $2,000 a day.

The worth-while changes in security prices do not generally occur within the same session. The market movement or the situation which produces it must have time in which to develop. As Charles Hayden once said to me, ''The day to buy is not the day to sell.''

Subscribers to *The Magazine* frequently write me and explain that they are far removed from the market and ask whether they had not better come to New York or go to Chicago so as to be in ''close touch with things.'' Very often this ''closeness'' is a handicap. One's real studying is done away from the market, not in a broker's office.

The best work I ever did in judging the market was when I devoted one hour a day in the middle of each session. I did not come to Wall Street. I had no news ticker. I seldom read the news items but judged solely from the action of the market itself; hence I was not influenced by any of the rumors, gossip, information or misinformation with which the Street is deluged day after day.

The out-of-town investor is therefore not under as much of a handicap as he might suppose. If he is trading and can get the result of the day's operation in time to give his orders next morning, he is better off than the majority of the people who come down here and hang over the ticker. His opinions are formed from the facts. He must know how to assemble these and draw the proper conclusions. But all he needs is the highest, lowest and last prices of the stocks which he is watching. Without being at all egotistical I believe I could go around the world and having arranged to have these few details of a stock like U. S. Steel or any other active issue cabled to me daily, I could cable my orders and come back with a profit. It would not be necessary for me to be advised of the volume of trading in that stock or the general market, although in some instances this might help. Certainly I would not care to have any news of any kind included in the cables.

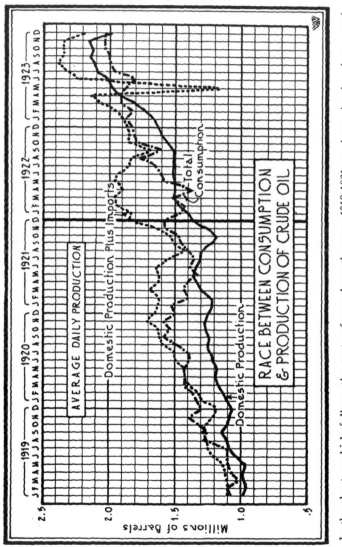

AVERAGE DAILY PRODUCTION

Domestic Production Plus Imports

Total Consumption

Domestic Production

RACE BETWEEN CONSUMPTION
& PRODUCTION OF CRUDE OIL

1919 1920 1921 1922 1923
JFMAMJJASOND

Millions of Barrels
2.5   2.0   1.5   1.0   .5

In the chapter which follows the text refers only to the years 1919-1921 as shown in the above graph

IX

I N previous chapters I have referred to the
value of foresight in the field of investment,
and the advantages of keeping your money
working where it will produce the best results
in the shortest time. I like to go cross-lots
toward an objective point. One way to do this
is to keep a constant eye on the relative position of the different industries in order to see
where the greatest advantage lies.

One hardly needs to do more than read the
papers nowadays to form the opinion that certain industries are in an excellent position.
But which of these is best?

The steel industry is apparently prosperous.
The industry seems likely to go through in a
belated way the filling of a vast commercial
and industrial vacuum which resulted from the
war's absorption of steel.

The resumption of building operations will

be a big factor in the steel business for the next several years. We all know that the country is underbuilt, and a revival of building activity which has of late become apparent, means very big things for the steel trade.

Now that the railroads are back in the hands of their owners we may expect increased orders for rails, cars and locomotives, all of which will absorb quantities of steel. This should also produce a highly prosperous condition in the railway equipment business for some years to come.

I have been turning these matters over in my mind recently because I am very confident of the future of the market and I want to know which stocks in the most favored industry are likely to produce the most for me both from the standpoint of income and profit. Market movements, when correctly forecasted, pay more dollars than dividends.

While there are many of the minor industries in a very favorable position at present, I have concluded that one in particular stands head and shoulders above all the rest and that is the petroleum industry. The accompanying graph indicates that consumption has run ahead of production for the past two years and there is no sign of any change in this trend. This, in conjunction with the forecast by Walter C. Teagle, president of the Standard Oil Co. of N. J., gives us the backbone of the statistical position of oil. Mr. Teagle estimates that by 1925 the world will require 675,000,000 bbls. of crude oil against 376,000,000 produced in 1920 —an increase of 78 per cent. He asks where such an enormous quantity of oil is coming from. If he cannot tell, you and I need not guess.

Should any further assurance be required, we can refer to a report filed by the British Board of Trade in London whose Central Committee reported that *demand* was tending to outstrip the world's present supply.

It is plain, therefore, that there is a threatened world shortage of oil and that this situation cannot be cured for a long time to come. I am therefore putting money into the best class of oil stocks, for while there are many promising opportunities in other fields I regard this, for the time being, as the best industry in which to take a substantial position on the long side.

My reason is that the margin of profit in the producing and refining of oil, especially the former, will be a very substantial one—probably much larger, figuring on a per share basis, than in the steel, equipment, automobile, or other of the leading industries whose output may be expanded by the building of more plants and hiring more men. It is different with the oil business. Oil must be sought; and it is not always to be found where you expect to find it. Many of the old fields are playing out. Many of the 10,000 and 15,000 barrel gushers of a year ago are now running in the dozens or hundreds and in not a few cases have to be pumped at that.

The Ranger Field on July 1, 1919, was producing 160,000 bbls. a day. By February 1, 1920, this had dropped to 80,000 barrels daily. The Burkburnett Field has shown a very marked falling off, due to close drilling. Many of the biggest wells in Mexico have declined, owing to economic conditions, salt water invasion, or possible change of formation, due to volcanic eruptions.

There is a scarcity of new fields. We hear about discoveries in various sections of this and other countries, but it will require a good many prolific fields to keep pace with the ravenous consumptive demand. It is apparent that in the oil industry there is no point of saturation, because the trade is continually working to make up a shortage which practically every year pulls down the visible supply.

The increase in the amount of machinery of all kinds and the elimination of hand labor is an important point in the demand, as each bit of machinery requires more lubrication and the lubricating material always has its base in crude oil. Automobiles are not only consumers of gasoline, but of great quantities of lubricating oil as well.

Tractors are developing another big new avenue of consumption and must in time supplant the horse on the farm, as the motor car has done in the cities. In Seattle there is not today a single horse, so far as I have been able to ascertain.

The year 1894 does not seem so long ago, yet when at that time I told some one that one of these days we would be traveling in horseless carriages, I was laughed at as being a dreamer.

Now I wish to record another similar dream.

It is that the streets of New York and all other great centers will, before many years, be underlaid with pipes which will carry fuel oil for use instead of coal in heating, manufacturing and other purposes. And here is a suggestion to any of my readers who are in a position to secure charters from their respective communities, for some day these charters will be worth a lot of money.

The day will soon pass when men shall be sent down into mines to haul up coal, put it on railroad trains, transport it hundreds of miles, unload it into coal carts, truck it through city streets, dump it into cellars and shovel it into furnaces.

Enormous oil tanks, similar to gas tanks now in use, should contain the liquid fuel which can be controlled by the mere turning of a valve or the operation of a thermostat.

No shovelling coal, or taking out ashes! This should make life in city or country more attractive, especially to those who have to hustle for the 5:15. But to the manufacturer, the owner of office buildings, or apartments, this development will have a much broader application, for it will mean the elimination of a number of factors that now contribute to the raising of rent, operating and manufacturing costs.

You may not follow this suggestion but somebody will, and a lot of somebodies will make a lot of millions in this way.

Practically every industry, from the peanut stand to the railroad locomotive and the enormous industrial plant, consumes oil in many ways. The world of machinery could not exist without oil. The use of machinery and particularly internal combustion motive power is spreading throughout the world. There are vast areas which are merely in the kerosene stage which will eventually be developed to the automobile and tractor stage. Carry the thought further and we see the likelihood that before many years we shall be shipping not only passengers but freight through the air, all of which means a still greater demand for crude oil to be converted into gasolene and lubricating oils.

These are some of the reasons why I have bought oil stocks during recent months. And why, in our Investment Letter, we have recommended these securities to our subscribers. By reason of the crying demand for crude, many of the refineries which have contracted to supply refined products are bidding against each other, so the companies which really hold the winning cards are the producers.

I anticipate a period of enormous profit-making in leading oil companies, particularly where they are intrenched in the field of production.

Most people make their mistake when averaging, by starting too soon; or, if they are buying on a close scale, say one point down, they do not provide sufficient capital to see them through in case the decline runs two or three times as many points as they anticipate. I recall a friend who, after seeing Union Pacific sell at 219 in August, 1909, thought it very cheap at 185 and much cheaper at 160. That made it a tremendous bargain at 135. He bought at all those figures. But at 116, his capital was exhausted, and, as they put it in Wall Street, "he went out with the tide."

X

A GREAT deal of money is lost or tied up by people who make a practice of averaging. Their theory is that if they buy a security at 100 and it goes to 90, it is that much cheaper, and the lower it goes the cheaper it grows. Like all Wall Street rules and theories, this is sometimes true; but there are a great many times when a security will decline in market price while its intrinsic value and earning power are shrinking even more swiftly.

While a decline in price is often due to a slump in the general market for bonds or stocks, or both, owing to some circumstance affecting a certain group of stocks, it also frequently occurs that the price is going down because of an inherent weakness in the company's affairs or a diminution of its prospects. Knowledge of such an influence is often confined to the few who are in close touch with the company's affairs. Sometimes there is a gradual development toward the unfavorable side; then again there may be an overnight happening which causes a radical change in former estimates or value.

Whatever the cause of a decline, the question of averaging is one that puzzles people who have bought at higher prices and are wondering whether averaging is not a good way out. Very often it proves to be the way to get in deeper. Hence, in order intelligently to judge whether to average, it is necessary to know what caused the decline.

I remember, a few years ago, buying a certain stock at around 45. Sometime after I bought it the price declined to about 30, at which point I afterward learned the stock was underwritten; so that to the insiders everything above 30 represented profit.

The company was doing a splendid business but the stock had been badly handled, and those who were responsible for its market action ran away and left the new baby on the public's door-step. Knowing that the stock was in the hands of the public, I did not average at 30, but waited until it was down to around 15. Then

I bought an equal amount. This I sold at ten points profit which marked my original cost down to $35. The stock then declined to 12 and I bought again, re-selling at 16, reducing my cost to about 31. Some months later it advanced to 38, where I sold. This let me out about even, allowing for interest.

These transactions ran over two or three years and serve to illustrate a good way of averaging out on a bond or stock which has been disappointing in its action. It is a method employed by large interests who, as previously described, often work on a much closer scale and take advantage of all the small variations in the market.

Why did I buy the stock when it was down? And why didn't I sell at a loss? Because I made investigations through the company's officials, and found that the corporation was in a very prosperous condition, having reduced its obligations and increased its earning power during the time when the stock was declining from 45 to a fraction of that figure. It was a case where intrinsic values were on the increase while the market price was decreasing.

Thus I kept myself always in a position where

I could buy more in case it went still lower and by selling on the rallies I provided the funds for repurchasing. Having bought the first lot (to average around 15) I was then in a position to sell it on a rally and re-buy it on a decline, so that whichever way the market went I would benefit. Had the price declined to 10 and then 5, I would probably have bought an equal amount or perhaps double the quantity at the low level—always with my eye on the compass, which was the company's physical, financial and commercial condition.

Stocks like this sometimes decline of their own technical weight, that is, the amount of shares that are pressing in liquidation, combined with an absence of support; or they may be put down—that is, artificially depressed by those who are desirous of accumulating at the low levels. In this case I believe there was a combination of both influences.

Most people make their mistake when averaging, by starting too soon; or, if they are buying on a close scale, say one point down, they do not provide sufficient capital to see them through in case the decline runs two or three times as many points as they anticipate.

I recall a friend who, after seeing Union Pacific sell at 219 in August, 1909, thought it very cheap at 185 and much cheaper at 160. That made it a tremendous bargain at 135. He bought at all those figures.   But at 116, his capital was exhausted and, as they put it in Wall Street, "He went out with the tide."

Eighty-five or ninety per cent. of the business, investment and speculative mortalities are due either to over-trading or lack of capital, which when boiled down are one and the same thing. And those who average their investment or speculative purchases supply in a great many instances, glaring examples of the causes of failure.

Years ago, when Weber & Fields formed one of the star theatrical attractions in New York, they used to have a scene in a bank where one of the team was the banker and the other the customer of the institution.

The "official" observing his "customer" at the wicket, made the very pertinent inquiry, "Put in or take out?"

I was reminded of this recently when thinking of the number of people who come down to the Street year after year, and with varying results (mostly bad, I must agree), keep on putting in and taking out until they either make a success or a failure of it. And I am continually asking myself, as a sort of test question, whether in putting in or taking out I am making progress or going backward. Like the frog who was trying to jump out of the well, I sometimes slip, but every year I can see that I am making progress.

There are seasons when it pays me to stick very close to shore, because, by reason of other influences, my judgment is not up to par. Sometimes, however, I am stubborn enough to keep on fighting through these periods, because no one can stay in the security market for a great many years without growing used to punishment. It has already been explained that success means more good than bad investments or ventures, so the readers of previous chapters will understand just what I mean.

Everyone should occasionally sit down and take account of stock—not securities, but his own ability, judgment, and what is most important, results thus far obtained. If he finds that the past few months or years have been unsatisfactory and unprofitable, judging from the amount of time, thought, study, and capital employed, he should suspend operations until he ascertains the cause; then he should set about to cure it. This can be done by study and practice (on paper or with ten share lots or single thousand dollar bonds if necessary) until he is confident that he has overcome the difficulty.

It may be that he is a chronic bull and finds himself in a bear market. I have frequently discovered that I was out of tune with the market, although I am never a *chronic* bull or bear, but always the kind of an animal the situation seems to call for.

It has been a great advantage to me, however, to have gone off by myself at times and figured out just where I stood, and, if things were going wrong, why? I find that it is more important to study my misfortunes than my triumphs.

JAMES R. KEENE

Who advised the "absolute limitation of risk" in market
operations. Keene was one of the shrewdest traders
Wall Street ever knew

XI

CONCLUSIONS AS TO FORESIGHT AND JUDGMENT

IT must be apparent from the foregoing chapters, that during the years I have spent in Wall Street I have not only kept my eyes and ears open, but have gained much as a result of study, practice and experience. It is logical to suppose that I have formed certain definite conclusions with regard to the business of trading and investing, and that these, if frankly and clearly stated and fully appreciated by those who read, should be of considerable value to the many who have not devoted so much time or effort in the same line of work.

No one can stay at it for even a short time without acquiring a certain knowledge, and it is for each to decide whether he is content to plod along in a desultory way, or go in for an intensive study of the subject. My recommendation to readers is that they take it up seriously. even if they have not a single dollar to invest at present.   The time will come when they will have funds for investment and the greater their store of information on the subject, the greater the incentive for saving or acquiring money in any legitimate way and the more profitable the outcome.

In an atmosphere of deceptive surface indications and false news, reports, gossip, methods, etc., such as one encounters in Wall Street, it is sometimes difficult to know just what one is trying to do and how well or how badly he is doing it.   It is not easy to size yourself up and to see just what are your basic principles, and how well you are following them.

Whenever a situation is not entirely clear to me, I find I can clarify it by putting down on paper all the facts, classifying them as favorable and unfavorable.   In thus writing it out on paper I not only have time to reason out each point as I go along, but when I get it all down it can be looked over and analyzed to much better advantage.

Following this idea I have written down perhaps fifty different conclusions which I have reached with regard to the business of trading and investing, and these I will take up, one after the other in this and later chapters, for they constitute a partial list of principles which should be recognized and applied, according to individual requirements.

These points are about equally divided between investment and speculation, but it is so difficult to determine where one begins and the other ends that in many cases I shall be obliged to treat them in combination. The thing we are trying to accomplish is an increase in our personal wealth, and whether this is done by the careful investment and slow accretion of money, the income of which is reinvested in order to enhance the principal sum, or whether we endeavor to increase our principal by attempting to forecast movements of security prices and to profit thereby—all that is something which each person must decide for himself.

BOTH MY PRIMARY AND MY ULTIMATE OBJECT IS THE SAFE AND PROFITABLE INVESTMENT OF MY FUNDS.

I say primary because that is my first and principal object and I use the term ultimate because eventually I expect to become an investor for income only. Provision for himself and family during the later years of his life is what every red-blooded man is working for. Some men—James R. Keene was one—continue to trade in stocks until they are very old. But most people want to feel that from at least sixty on they will be free from the necessity of making money on which to live during their declining years.

Trading profits should therefore be used to increase the principal sum which is invested in income-bearing securities, preferably those which will grow in market value. Income from such investments should be made to compound itself by re-investing it as received.

IF ONE IS NOT ADAPTED TO TRADING HE SHOULD PROVE IT TO HIS OWN SATISFACTION AND THEN ABANDON THE BUSINESS.—He should then attempt to become an intelligent and successful investor. Failing of this, he should turn to savings banks and mortgages or other non-fluctuating mediums for the investment of his funds.

A friend of mine once had something over $100,000 worth of bonds, a few of which he deposited with a broker as margin. The bonds were his backlog; they represented the result of his savings from the time he first entered business, and were bringing in a good income, besides having possibilities.   As he traded back and forth, he found that he was gradually taking some of the bonds which he had in his box, and putting them up with the broker, until finally he reached a point where nearly half of the bonds were gone.   This, he decided, was conclusive evidence of the fact that he was not adapted to the business of trading.   He therefore discontinued trading and resumed the saving tactics by which he had accumulated the first hundred bonds.

That was some years ago.   He has now over $200,000 worth, and when at rare intervals he ventures into the speculative arena, he does it very timidly and with only trifling sums.

I recommend this man's course to those who have had similar experiences, but with this exception: If they are willing to devote themselves to the task, they will doubtless overcome their difficulties and be more successful with the added study and experience.   But to go right on putting good money after bad, not only reflects on a man's business judgment but indicates a weakness in his character which he had best conquer in short order.

The experiences of our earlier years are well and cheaply bought if we really profit by them.

No one can avoid having his capital tied up at times in mediums which are not satisfactory. But there should be no hesitation about switching, even though it necessitates the taking of a loss in your present holdings. A good security will make up this loss much faster than one which is mediocre. So the question which one should ask himself with relation to all of the securities which he holds, is this: "Are there any other issues which will work for me more profitably and in a shorter time than these? I cannot afford to let money sleep, nor have it work slowly. I am like a merchant: I must turn my money over as often as I can, so that the average yearly return will be at its maximum."

One's Capital Should Be Made to Do the Greatest Service in the Shortest Length of Time.—This applies both to trading capital and investment capital. I have found that it is best to use only a small part of the total available capital for trading. To employ all or most of it is a fatal mistake, for in case of an unforeseen situation, causing a large loss, one is obliged to begin over again; whereas if the bulk of the capital is invested where it is safe, returns an income, and will probably enhance in value, then in case of a calamity a part of it can be turned into cash in order to renew trading operations.

But this should occur in only rare instances. When a man finds that he has a certain sum invested and that this sum is diminishing on account of his pulling it down for trading purposes, he is on the wrong track and had better stop short and take account of himself before he travels further.   A person who cannot be successful in trading with a small amount of capital, will unquestionably lose a large amount if he employs it.

In making one's capital do the greatest amount of work in the shortest length of time, it is necessary to be forever on the lookout for better opportunities than those which you now have.   If you hold bonds which are selling between 90 and 95, and which may, in a good bond market, advance to 110, you would not be justified in retaining them if you can buy another bond which is just as well secured, just as marketable, and has all the other good points of your present security, besides being convertible into a security which has excellent prospects of an advance to a very much higher figure.

Should you own a preferred stock which is paying its 7 per cent. and showing on the average only one and a half times its dividends, whereas you can buy, at the same price, another preferred stock which is earning three or four times its dividend, taking the average of a number of years, it is by all means best to make the exchange. It is highly important to find out just what we can and cannot do, but we should not be discouraged too soon. I have met thousands and thousands of people who were endeavoring to make money in speculation and regret to say that very few are really qualified to become successful traders of any importance.

But there are hundreds of thousands of successful investors, and it is toward this avenue of success and independence that I hope to turn the attention of most of my readers. By studying "the public" and its ways, I have learned what kind of operations the majority are best fitted for; while it is a peculiar fact that very few people delude themselves into thinking that they are good physicians, surgeons, lawyers or dentists, they do try to fool themselves into believing that they are good investors and speculators.

Look around you—do you find that among your acquaintances 100% are well-to-do and successful business men? Are not the majority just plodding along, neither getting rich nor poor? Well, that is just as true in Wall Street as it is in business. You can generally pick the brilliant successes and count them on the fingers of one or both hands, depending on the size of your circle of acquaintances.

People are successful in business because, while they make mistakes at first, they study these mistakes and avoid them in future. Then by gradually acquiring a knowledge of the basic principles of success, they develop into good business men. But how many apply this rule to their investing and trading? Very few do any studying at all. Very few take the subject seriously. They drift into the security market, very often "get nipped," as the saying is, avoid it for a while, return from time to time with similar results, then gradually drift away from it, without ever having given themselves a chance to develop into what might be good traders or intelligent investors.

This is all wrong. People go seriously into the study of medicine, the law, dentistry, or they take up with strong purpose the business of manufacturing of merchandising, but very few ever go deeply into this vital subject which should be seriously undertaken by all.

Now we all admit that the average man is mentally lazy. He hates work, mental or physical, doesn't want to spend an hour every evening, or even once a week, except at bridge, poker, or something else equally diverting and interesting. Those who do employ their time profitably are headed toward wealth and independence; but in many cases the poker players will later be supported by their children.

But to return to our subject, it should not take more than a few years for a person to find out whether he is qualified for trading or whether he should devote himself to the investment side of the proposition.

THE CULTIVATION OF FORESIGHT IS MOST ESSENTIAL.—In the main it is the man with the greatest amount of foresight who is most suc-

cessful in the security market. Foresight is
the very essence of speculation. Without the
use of it a person is not speculating at all—
he is merely taking chances—gambling.

One of the late J. P. Morgan's strong points
was his ability to foresee and therefore to anticipate the vast changes in financial conditions
and security prices. It was marvelous how he
frequently predicted, months in advance, the
outcome of certain involved business and financial situations which were not understood or
anticipated by anyone else. This was one of
the qualities that made him great. It enabled
him to engage in vast undertakings, of which the
U. S. Steel Corporation is a conspicuous example, but there are many other industrial mon-
uments to his financial genius which was, after
all, built around his marvelous foresight.

It was foresight which made E. H. Harriman
a great man. It enabled him to anticipate the
development of the Union Pacific and Southern
Pacific Railroads and nerved him to undertake
the stupendous task of creating a railroad em-
pire.

Harriman once held an ordinary job—just
like you and I once did, or do now—and if he,

through the cultivation of foresight, and the other qualities which made him pre-eminent, could accomplish such splendid results, then you and I can, by the exercise of the talents with which we are blessed, advance our personal fortunes by concentrating on the development of our own foresight. It will prove of value, not only in our investments, but in every undertaking which we enter—financial, business or personal—during our whole lives. So let us give close attention to the subject. A large part of such success as I have already attained is due to my having formed the habit of looking ahead to see in what direction future events are likely to run.

IT IS BETTER TO DEPEND ON YOUR OWN JUDGMENT THAN ON THAT OF ANY OTHER PERSON.— If you have not reached a point where you can do this, better continue your studies and practice until you can form a sound, independent judgment on which you can base your commitments.

We hear a great deal in Wall Street about "inside information" and the value of big connections. But I have found that the man who depends the most on his own judgment is headed for success if he has not already attained it.   It is very easy to be swayed by the multitudinous opinions that are bandied around the Street and which may be had for nothing because they are generally worth it.

Suppose you are a most intimate personal friend of a man who is putting through a big deal in a security which is listed on the New York Stock Exchange.   He tells you all the facts and puts you in a position to buy, with a thorough knowledge of what is going on.   You do buy, and perhaps you make money, but more often than not it will turn out when you come to realize, you will be so enthused by your inside knowledge that you will not sell at the right time, or a hitch will occur which turns your profit into a loss, or your big man is out of town, or something is happening to the market which he cannot explain.

But suppose you do get away with a profit— you are apt to be so carried off your feet that at your very next opportunity you will think you have Wall Street by the tail and will plunge with all you have made and all you have besides, and eventually end up with a loss.   The kind of money which does you the most good is that which you make through your own efforts. All Wall Street is trying to get something for nothing. Don't join the crowd. Rather, "buck it"—the crowd is generally wrong. Become one of the successful few who build stone upon stone until they have a solid foundation of knowledge and experience which will last them all their lives.

If I believed that the people who are now reading and studying the numerous articles which appear in *The Magazine* would, five or ten years from now, still be looking to it for easy ways to make money, I should be very much discouraged. But if, as I believe, a great many will, through its teachings, be induced to become students and ultimately intelligent and successful investors, then I will feel that the many years of hard work which I have put into the publication have been well rewarded.

Down in New Street, on the block between Wall Street and Exchange Place, you will find, on any pleasant day, a lot of Wall Street "Ghosts" sunning themselves. And by way of explanation let me say that a Wall Street Ghost is one who has tried to make money in the market and failed. He is the saddest sight in all the financial district.   Once a prosperous and perhaps wealthy business man, he is now reduced to mere driftwood among the eddies which surround the Stock Exchange.   In and out of the brokerage offices you find him rambling in a hopeless fashion, always on the lookout for "tips."   The red-headed bootblack and Jim, the shoe-lace man, are types of his confidants.   He always know where everything is going, but never gets anywhere himself.

I don't know what becomes of these old "Ghosts" who drift about the old stamping ground, but it is instructive to know that their ranks are recruited from the people who never tried to cultivate a judgment of their own, but always depended on that of others.

THE LONGER YOUR EXPERIENCE, THE BETTER BACKGROUND YOU HAVE FOR COMPARISON, AND THE GREATER YOUR ABILITY TO JUDGE AND FORECAST CORRECTLY.—As conditions are constantly changing, no two markets are alike and no two daily sessions are similar; but markets and sessions and panics and booms all have certain characteristics which should be carefully studied and intimately understood.

The man who has never been through a panic

would be apt to find himself badly rattled. Under a pressure of excitement and nervous strain he would probably do the wrong thing. But anyone who has experienced a number of panics, knows how to conduct his operations so as to take the utmost advantage of such a rare opportunity, provided he has previously put himself in a position to buy at the low prices.

To some people it may be discouraging to say that you must keep at this business for many years in order to become highly successful; but is not this what you must do in your own line of business? Are not the best business and professional men those who have had the longest practice?

You cannot go into any phase of endeavor and make money or become prominent "just like that"—you must serve your apprenticeship. Of course, if you want to join the ranks of the large percentage of people who spend their declining years in the care or custody of their children or relatives, or in institutions, then you can afford to ignore my suggestion that work and study and long experience are essential. But if you have imagination and can picture yourself as possessing wealth and contentment in your old age, you will immediately admit that it is well worth your while to devote serious attention to this subject.

You have to live anyhow, so why not live well? It all depends on you, for you can generally take out in as great a measure as you put in.

By long experience I do not mean merely reading the financial columns for thirty or forty years; one does not gain experience in that way. I refer to the practical experience of investing in stocks and bonds; making mistakes; finding out why and profiting thereby in future.

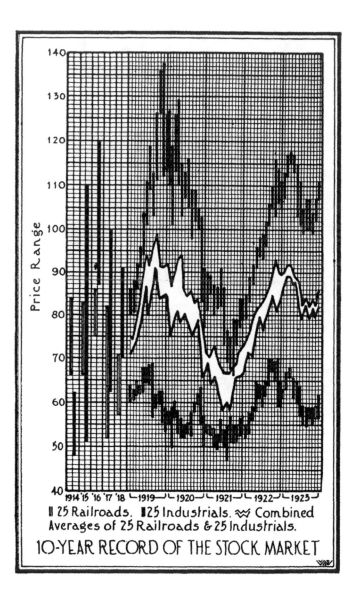

Price Range

140

130

120

110

100

90

80

70

60

50

40

1914 '15 '16 '17 '18 1919 1920 1921 1922 1923

▌▌ 25 Railroads. ▌ 25 Industrials. ≈ Combined
Averages of 25 Railroads & 25 Industrials.

10-YEAR RECORD OF THE STOCK MARKET

XII

SAFEGUARDING YOUR CAPITAL

THE question is not whether you can make money with your original capital but whether you will cease because of the loss of this initial money at the very outset.

There is everything in getting a good start. In a preceding chapter it was shown that I did not begin to invest until eight years after my studies had commenced, and that I did not begin trading until six years after that. Just how long the average investor should pursue his studies without putting his ideas into practical operation is a matter for each individual to decide, but there should be a thorough understanding of the theoretical side before the first ventures or investments are actually made.

A person becomes competent in other fields because he has generally gone through a long period of practice and preparation. A physician for example, goes to college, attends clinics, rides in an ambulance, serves in hospitals, and, after some years of preparatory work, hangs out a sign. In Wall Street the same M.D. would hang out his sign first; then proceed to practice. In one way the doctor's work, in and out of Wall Street, bears resemblance, inasmuch as when he begins to practice his profession he has to acquire patients. In Wall Street it is spelled "patience." Both are absolutely necessary to his success.

The Magazine of Wall Street has often repeated warnings against beginning to operate before you know how; but the truth will bear many repetitions, and as our circle of readers is constantly widening we are again emphasizing this point.

If Wall Street could only retain the same clientele year after year and add to it the many who for the first time find themselves with investment or trading capital, we should have four million and five million share days instead of one and two million. It is strange that in the financial district, which is the very heart of the nation's commercial and industrial structure, there is such a woeful lack of understanding of what the public requires in the way of assistance.

My organization has devoted a great deal of effort to showing the brokerage houses that in order to permanently retain their clients, steps should be taken to educate them. We have offered to sell the banking, brokerage and investment houses quantities of literature at cost and have tried to show the brokerage fraternity how important it is to disseminate educational books and pamphlets on this subject, in order that their clients, through genuine knowledge, might become permanent instead of transient, patrons of their respective houses. But with rare exceptions, our appeals have fallen upon ears that were deaf. Brokers would rather go on securing, at great expense, new clients to take the place of those who become discouraged and fall by the wayside. Some day a brokerage house will be evolved which has, as a permanent part of its organization, an educational department whose business it will be to see that its clients are properly informed as to just what they should do and how they should do it. Meantime, the individual investor is deprived of assistance from the logical source whence it should come.

The people who really stay at the business and continue year after year to buy and sell securities can generally be classified into two divisions. First, those who have outside sources of income and are continually bringing money into the street, and, second, those who are successful in their operations and thereby increase their capital, or to a greater or lesser extent maintain themselves out of what they thus realize. It is unfortunate that the percentage of those who bring money to Wall Street is so large and that many do not realize that it is their lack of knowledge and their inefficient methods in the financial field which bring such unsatisfactory results.

Lawyers, doctors, surgeons and other professional men are obliged, under state laws, to pass certain examinations and receive certificates showing that they are competent to practice. This is for the protection of the public, but no way has been provided whereby the public can be protected against its own operations in the security market. It would be a good thing if the financial lives of more customers of brokerage houses could be sustained by making them pass an examination as to knowledge of the subject and ability to take care of themselves. Many states require applicants to pass an examination before they are given permission to drive an automobile on the public highways. In one case it is a physical and in the other a financial risk.

A certain amount of mistakes and a percentage of unfortunate investments are to be expected, no matter how well you start or how expert you become. But you should always preserve your trading or investment capital by never putting yourself in a position to have this wiped out. As the Irishman said, "It is betther to be hurted than kilt." Lack of capital and over-trading, being the cause of most misfortunes, are the result of being too heavily committed in one direction or another.

Investors who begin with even a single one hundred dollar capital have the choice of being conservative or of over-trading, but through ignorance many do not realize just when they are over-reaching and when their operations may be designated as conservative. In order to avoid a danger, they must know where it lies. It would be foolish for a corporal to lead an army into a strange country; and just as foolish for any novice to marshal his capital and launch into one or another phase of buying or selling stocks or bonds, without previous study.

A cross-section of the public's operations would show lack of interest when prices are low and the market is dragging along. When prices begin to advance the public begins to buy and this buying increases in proportion to the extent and rapidity of the advance until, at the top of an important movement, the public is 95% bullish and, as a rule, loaded up. The more uninterrupted the advance, the greater and more rapid the increase in public commitments.

Examining the cross-section in a panic we would find that those who went heavily long on the way up and at the top are selling out or being sold out. The buying is by new recruits, consisting of bargain-hunting people who have never before bought securities, combined with the comparatively few who sold while prices

were high, and who therefore have money to
invest.

Prices may have advanced steadily for a
couple of years prior to the panic and those
who began with a small amount of capital may
have accumulated good round sums when
figured at the high prices—mostly paper profits. But as bear markets are generally both
swift and severe, these profits are quickly swept
away, so that often those who have been piling
them up for two years often lose them in thirty
or sixty days.

You may say to yourself: "Oh, well, the
public may do that, but I'm not one of the public." But the fact is, unless you are a trained
and experienced trader or investor, or have, to
some extent, a claim to being an insider, a professional or semi-professional, then you are
one of that vast majority which constitutes the
great American speculative and investing public. The sooner you realize this fact the more
quickly you can adjust yourself to your proper
position in the financial scale.

The point of difference between the public
and those who are not of this class is found in

the fact that the public is not sophisticated; in other words, not trained in the business. If you are trained, you are not a member of that body.

Having thus classified yourself it is your business to ascertain how you can proceed without danger to the point where you can safely and profitably depend upon your own judgment. My personal opinion is that this can best be done by a course of study before beginning operations, because a satisfactory outcome is the result of knowledge plus capital. If you lack either the knowledge or the capital or both you cannot succeed, so the logical course is to get the knowledge first, meanwhile saving or setting aside the capital.

It is stupidity which makes people "rush in where angels fear to tread." And there is something about the Wall Street atmosphere which makes people think that whatever is to be done must be done at once, otherwise the opportunity will get away from them. I find that opportunities are coming along all the time, and that the majority are not as good as they look. So the best ones are worth waiting for.

The young man with his first money might very well spend his spare time for five years in study, investigation, self-training, in order to find out whether he is an investor, a trader, or a speculator, and the more he learns about it the greater he will realize how very ignorant he was at the beginning. If, at the age of thirty, he sees the necessity for study, and at thirty-five he has accumulated some capital which in the meantime has been reposing in the savings banks or in high grade bonds or mortgages, he should not even then go in with the idea of cleaning up a fortune, but with intent to cautiously and conservatively proceed, so that during the entire balance of his life he will steadily build up his fund of investment knowledge and capital on a constantly broadening base.

This matter is not anything that has to be hustled—you can pursue your regular business with this as a side line or hobby, if you like. You can't learn everything in a minute, but of course the more time you can devote to it the more rapidly you can proceed to practice.

The main point, as I have said, is to so preserve your initial capital that you will never be deprived of it, and the way to do this is to learn what you are about before you go about it.

It is well to study the methods of other large and successful operators and investors.

Much can be learned from this source. There is great value in imitation, but of course we must select the individuals whose methods have been scientific and whose results speak for themselves.

When I was a small boy I became interested in the study of music. Some of my teachers were better qualified than others, but the one under whom I made the most progress was the one who interested me in the broad aspect of the art by inducing me not merely to practice hard but to attend the best of concerts and operas; to study the theory of music, the history of great composers, the characteristics of great compositions, the principles of harmony, etc. This teacher would, when I was learning a particularly difficult passage on the piano or organ, sit down and play it for me so that I could imitate. The result was that I became so interested in my lessons that I devoted to them practically all of my spare time and money.

That is the way to go into this subject. While you cannot expect big financiers or large and successful traders to sit down and tell you just how they do it, there is, in these enlightened days, a world of literature bearing on the subject. Past volumes of *The Magazine* contain many articles of this nature. Your public libraries are all supplied with helpful material. Many hints are to be derived from a study of the methods of successful men.

"There is no place in the modern world for the unskilled; no one can hope for any genuine success who fails to give himself the most complete special education. Good intentions go for nothing, and industry is thrown away if one cannot infuse a high degree of skill into his work. The trained man has all the advantages on his side; the untrained man invites all the tragic possibilities of failure."

XIII

MANY years ago there was a stock dealt in on the New York Curb called Arlington Copper. The "mine" was said to be over a hundred years old and, with the modern methods which could be applied to the low-grade ore in the property, the promoters claimed they would be able to make a very big profit.

The seat of this operation was at Arlington, N. J., a small residential town just across the meadows from Jersey City. One could step on an Erie train and be there in twenty minutes. He could have seen a lot of old workings, and a lot of rock that was pointed out as ore. The round trip might have cost a dollar and occupied three hours.

Did any of the people who eagerly purchased the stock on the Curb take a trip over to Arlington to see what they were buying? They

did not. They were "too busy," or they had
to be home at 6:30, as they had a "dinner en-
gagement." Possibly their meal time or their
evening's social affair was more important than
the many thousands of dollars which they put
into this stock, but in any event Arlington Copper passed away as many "good things" are
apt to do.

One does not have to look far to find
many illustrations of this point. The public
does not investigate, but buys and sells on somebody's say-so, and without using the precau-
tions that would surely be applied in its own
particular line of business.

For many years I have been impressed with
the necessity of having investigation precede
investments, instead of succeeding them. Take
the field of patents and calculate, if you can,
how many hundreds of millions are sunk each
year in somebody's new-fangled idea as to how
this or that should be done. In discussing this
matter with an expert mechanical engineer the
other day, it developed that 97% of the patents
that are taken out are either of no commercial
value or are never developed to a point where
they realize a profit. Yet, as he said, "There

are many big men in this town whose ear you can get quicker with a new patented appliance than in any other way. They will lay aside their own line of business and take up your new mechanism, if it is something that tickles their fancy.'' But that is only one field.

It is impossible to estimate how many hundreds of millions are lost because of improper preliminary investigation of the commercial, financial and technical aspects of the enterprises which absorb such a large proportion of the public wealth. Yet there is no other way in which money may be so intelligently spent as in safeguarding capital.

Most people do not know how to investigate an enterprise. Some one comes along with a newly patented washing machine. He needs $25,000 to ''develop it.'' He would like to get you and some of your friends to put up $5,000 each. He will give you 51% interest in the business. He invites investigation. But you and your friends do not really investigate—you get hold of somebody who is already in the washing machine business and ask what he thinks of it. He is not an expert; he doesn't know the patent situation—all he knows is whether he can sell the machine he is now handling and whether he thinks this is better than his, but he has no broad understanding of the business because all he is handling is one little machine in one little corner of the U. S. A.   A few hundred or a few thousand dollars spent in a thorough investigation would save a lot of trouble, time and money.

The same principle applies to an oil, mining, railroad, industrial, or any other kind of enterprise.   Money spent in careful investigation is insurance against loss.   It is also productive of information which will be valuable in case you desire to go into the business or buy shares.

An enterprise in which I have an interest has recently decided to put a new product on the market.   The demand had been established and greatly exceeded the supply.   There was no question as to the company's ability to make the goods and sell them, but there was a question as to just what grade of goods would best please the public and just how they should be sold.   So a very broad survey of the whole industry was ordered, with the result that the company is now in a position to go forward with its new goods in an intelligent way, along the line of least resistance. It is this sort of pre-vision which makes for success.

It is a remarkable and confirmatory fact that the officials of this company frequently take speculative fliers and make investments in securities, but their investigations seldom go beyond the stage of a surface inquiry as to the opinion of one or two parties, including the broker who is at the other end of the telephone listening for an order.

That reminds me of a point I have often made as to the ethics involved, in the client asking and the broker giving an opinion as to a contemplated investment or speculation. Personally, I believe that the client should know what he wants to do before he approaches the broker and that the latter's function is to execute the order and finance the operation. Many people do not agree with me, but it is a matter which we may take up for discussion at another time.

Perhaps you cannot investigate personally, owing to lack of time or knowledge of the subject, but you can always secure the services of those who can. In one of my previous chapters I stated some of my experiences in mining

stocks and showed how I employed mining engineers to examine properties and other engineers to check them up. Mining is only one
form of industry which is represented in Wall
Street, and I should say that there are many,
many more enterprises besides mines that need
investigation. Within the past several months
a number of propositions have been shown up
as representing but a fraction of the value originally claimed for them by the promoters.

What Wall Street needs is some means of
"checking up" on the enthusiasm and, in some
cases, the deception of those who are engaged in
marketing securities. There are two kinds of
people in the financial district: those who are
trying to help themselves by helping others, and
those who are helping themselves to what others
possess. It does not take long to find out
whether those with whom you are dealing belong to the preferred class.

Investigation of some of the enterprises
whose securities are dealt in, is a subject calling
for a very wide range of knowledge and ability,
and is beyond the reach of the average man.
An examination of a property like the Philadelphia Company, for example, or Cities Serv-

ice or Ohio Cities Gas would require training in a great many different fields, many of which the average investor does not understand. A thorough investigation of such an enterprise would only be justified by a very large investment.

It is for this reason that such a large percentage of people who buy securities are stockholders in U. S. Steel, because the steel business is something they understand, or think they do, and the Steel Corporation is a leader in the frequency and detail of its periodical reports, containing essential statistics of which almost anybody can understand the main features. If some other corporations with complex organizations would make their operations so well understood to the average investor, and by past performances attain such a degree of confidence in the minds of the public, many people might sell their U. S. Steel and buy the other securities. But with the Steel Corporation occupying a position of prominence similar to a mountain surrounded by little hills, it is easy for any one to see just where the mountain stands and its relative breadth and height compared with its neighbor's.

The more I study this subject, the greater appears the necessity for "investigation before investing." In the matter of discrimination alone there is such a wide range of conditions and so many angles from which comparisons may be made, that the subject is, except in some instances, highly complicated and calls for a clear and expert judgment before deciding upon a definite course.

Next in importance to knowing what to buy is the question as to when it should be done.

I was discussing this matter with an investor today. He referred to the assets and earning power of a big corporation whose securities had recently suffered a very material decline. He could not understand why the stock should go down in the face of such a showing of commercial and financial strength.

My answer was this: "You have an automobile—it consists of a lot of steel, wood, rubber, brass, leather and other material. It requires gasoline, water, air and lubricating oil. Also knowledge as to how to adjust the whole piece of complicated machinery so that all the parts will work harmoniously. The smallest thing about your automobile is the spark.   Without it the whole mass becomes junk.   With the spark at least you can get the machinery to go, and you might plug along.   But: Unless your spark is *timed* to fire at the exact moment when the piston reaches a certain point of elevation in the cylinder, you might as well get out and walk.

"It is the same way with the stock which you just mentioned.   The company has ample working capital, high class management, big earning power, wonderful prospects.   It is probably in a better and stronger position than when its stock sold thirty points higher.   In this case the 'spark' is represented by the technical position.   At 140 the spark was not properly adjusted.   At 110 the adjustment has improved, but a study of the technical position of this stock will eventually point out the exact moment when it should be bought; so get all your other factors lined up ready for the time when the technical position shows that it is time to buy."

In the fluctuations of almost every security **there** comes a time when it may be most advantageously bought or sold, and the training of one's judgment in the making of decisions as to "when," is one of the fine points in the business. It is also one of the least understood.

Certain "authorities" on securities and their markets have very frequently been proven to be badly wrong, principally because they have ignored this important consideration. They may as well ignore the trigger in a gun.

Carnegie's advice: "Put all your eggs in one basket and then watch the basket" might apply to an industrial organization of which he was the head, but it does not apply generally in the field of investment.

One's holdings should be so diversified by commitments in various lines of business, in different localities and subject to dissimilar influences, that no matter what happens, only a small portion of the investment is affected.

Before the Spanish War, our warships used to carry an observation tower which consisted of one solid piece of steel so constructed that a well-directed shot would demolish it, but during the war some bright mind in the navy conceived the idea of a tower consisting of a network of steel strips which took fifteen or more shots in certain spots to knock it down, and thus was the factor of safety vastly increased.

Investors should follow out this plan of protecting themselves by a diversification of investments, just as an insurance company avoids the risking of its capital and surplus on a single building. By spreading its risk over a vast number of buildings in various localities, it is protecting itself against a catastrophe.

Whatever the sum invested, it should be spread among at least ten to twenty different securities, greatly contrasting each other in nature of business, margin of safety, location of the industry, etc. Thus will your funds be hedged about with protection against shrinkage. And in the search for proper mediums you will widen your knowledge by a careful and discriminating study of the subject.

When you stop to think of it, you will see that it is impossible for all securities to have equal value and prospects; therefore some must be better than others. To be able to select the few which are absolutely the best requires a very broad knowledge and great statistical and analytical training and capability. The possession of such qualifications, however, enables one to go cross lots toward his goal of sound investments and money making.

XIV

I T is important to know whether large operators, inside interests, a pool, or the public dominate the market for a certain security or group.

You have often heard the expression, "Stocks are in weak hands." It is a matter of almost decisive importance to know where the stocks making up the leading group of speculative shares or any single security are held.

The reason this is so important is as follows: A combination of bankers will seldom be found on the long side of the market unless they expect a pronounced change in security market conditions in the near future. Their own purchases, therefore, are an indication of probable betterment. When a pool takes hold, it is usually in a certain one or a few issues which are likely to be favorably affected by developments known to a few but not generally known. The same is true of a large individual operator, who takes a position with a big line of stocks because he is confident that the future will cause others to take the securities off his hands at higher levels.

Operations on such a scale are very often the deciding factors in the trend of the market, because of the great quantities of securities which are dealt in.   Such purchases exhaust the floating supply and thus lead to a higher level. Large interests and operators also have a way of influencing the market in the desired direction.   This we may term manipulation, or advertising, or marking up, or whatever we choose, but it remains a fact, nevertheless, that this is frequently done.   Some people claim that there is a "power" which dominates the market, and perhaps this is true to a degree, but not in the sense that many believe.   Large interests sometimes work together, or observe each other's attitude by the action of their respective stocks, and thus operate in harmony, but without any actual understanding.

There is, however, another group of people operating in the market almost constantly, and this group is really the largest and most power-

fui of all. I refer to the investment and speculative public which is, in most cases, untrained, and as a body is unorganized. If the
public could get together and operate in harmony so that it would not continually be step-
ping on its own toes, there would be a different
kind of Wall Street; for without the public as
a buffer, large interests, pools and operators
would be comparatively powerless.

Some may criticize this statement on the
ground that it is made offhand and without any
definite proof, but I have had occasion in the
past to prove that it is true, and do not consider
it necessary to present the facts here. The report of the committee appointed in 1909 by
Governor Hughes for the purpose of investigating the workings of the New York Stock
Exchange, published in *The Magazine* for August, 1909, refers to the operations of the floor
traders, who, "from their familiarity with the
technique of dealings on the Exchange and their
ability to act in concert with others and thus
manipulate values, are supposed to have special
advantages over other traders."

I claim that if a few floor traders, properly
organized, can get results, the public could,

properly organized, control the situation. I merely mention this to illustrate the point that the big thing to know is where the stocks are, because the position of those who control is an indication of their attitude, pose and power.

It will be admitted that some years ago—before the railroads were persecuted and their profits curtailed by innumerable anti-railroad organizations—their securities were largely held by the great banking interests, each controlling its respective groups of securities. The Rockefellers were in St. Paul, New Haven and others, Harriman and Kuhn-Loeb interests in control of the Union Pacific, Southern Pacific, etc., and the Morgans dominated their specialties. But a change has come over the situation, and now I may safely make the statement that the great bulk of shares of the American railroads are in the hands of small investors.

Large interests got out long ago. They saw the handwriting on the wall; they had a right to sell and protect themselves and they did sell. The big ten thousand, fifty thousand and hundred thousand share blocks were split up into small lots and are so held today. The ten share owner is now more representative of railroad control that at any time in the history of the world and this situation will continue until there is a very radical change in the outlook for the American railroad industry.

Having satisfied myself that this is the situation, I am in a better position to judge the action of the market for these stocks and to decide upon my individual course, so far as I care to trade or invest in the rails. There are exceptions to this rule, but it is safe to say that outside the individual movements in special issues or groups, there is not likely to be any concerted action until large interests see clearly that the future will be brighter and better, otherwise they would not be justified in accumulating.

When this accumulation begins, as it probably will, sooner or later, there will be a very distinct change in the character of the market for railroad stocks. That change will first evince itself in the transactions.

It will be seen from the above how important it is to know who holds the stocks, and how the public, unorganized, is incapable of applying anything but a superficial aid in the dull, dragging, declining markets we have had in this group.

This being the case, the bankers, large operators and pools, are looking elsewhere for their security market profits.

There are some opportunities that are better than any others offering at the moment. One's task is to ferret these out.

It is astonishing how many people in Wall Street work on "hunches." Whenever your friend tells you about the splendid profits he realized in certain transactions, he is almost certain to tell you, "I had a hunch that it was a purchase at that price." But when a loss results from some of his ventures, he does not lay it to a "hunch" but to "hard luck."

People are apt to conduct their investments a good deal as advertising was conducted in former years, when the advertiser's theory was, "put an ad. in the paper and see how you come out." To quote from a very interesting address by Mr. M. H. Avram, "Advertising is no longer a hit or miss proposition—it is scientifically conducted and executed along previously determined and experience-proven lines.   An advertising campaign may deviate at times as to details, due to circumstances that could not be forseen, but in its fundamentals the predetermined line is followed unwaveringly toward success.''

In other words, advertising—formerly a very inexact science—has become scientific. It is quite within the bounds of possibility that investing may also be put on the same plane. We are making slow but steady progress toward that end.

In writing this book I have endeavored to give examples as to how some of the difficulties in this big subject can be overcome and the last few chapters have been devoted to observations which may help to solve some of these questions.   I do not wish to close without saying a word in favor of the careful selection of investment mediums.

As stated at the beginning of this subject, there are some opportunities that are better than any others.   When you stop to think of it, you will see that it is impossible for all securities to have equal value and prospects; therefore some must be better than others.   To be able to select the few which are absolutely the best requires a very broad knowledge and great statistical and analytical training and capability. The possession of such qualifications, however, enables one to go cross-lots toward his goal of sound investments and money-making.

It is a deeply interesting subject. The more you learn, the more you realize how little you know, and the more anxious you become to acquire proficiency.

While as a nation we are perhaps becoming more studious, we are also more pleasure-loving. And one's desire to study and advance is often handicapped by the influences which pull him toward pastimes and recreation. An engineer friend of mine tells me that he never goes to sleep without reading on some educational subject for at least half an hour. This habit, now thoroughly formed, has been of inestimable value to him in his practice. His example may be imitated to very great advantage.

THE END

COSIMO-on-DEMAND

COSIMO is an innovative publisher of books and publications that inspire, inform and engage readers worldwide. Our titles are drawn from a range of subjects including health, business, philosophy, history, science and sacred texts. We specialize in using print-on-demand technology (POD), making it possible to publish books for both general and specialized audiences and to keep books in print indefinitely. With POD technology new titles can reach their audiences faster and more efficiently than with traditional publishing.

> **Permanent Availability:** Our books & publications never go out-of-print.

> **Global Availability:** Our books are always available online at popular retailers and can be ordered from your favorite local bookstore.

COSIMO CLASSICS brings to life unique, rare, out-of-print classics representing subjects as diverse as *Alternative Health, Business and Economics, Eastern Philosophy, Personal Growth, Mythology, Philosophy, Sacred Texts, Science, Spirituality* and much more!

COSIMO-on-DEMAND publishes your books, publications and reports. If you are an Author, part of an Organization, or a Benefactor with a publishing project and would like to bring books back into print, publish new books fast and effectively, would like your publications, books, training guides, and conference reports to be made available to your members and wider audiences around the world, we can assist you with your publishing needs.

Visit our website at www.cosimobooks.com to learn more about Cosimo, browse our catalog, take part in surveys or campaigns, and sign-up for our newsletter.

And if you wish please drop us a line at info@cosimobooks.com. We look forward to hearing from you.

Printed in the United States
113349LV00001B/61/A

9 781596 050778